ELECTRONICS
FOR YOUNG PEOPLE

New Fourth Edition

Also by Jeanne Bendick

ALL AROUND YOU

HAVE A HAPPY MEASLE

HOW MUCH AND HOW MANY

TELEVISION WORKS LIKE THIS, *Third Rev. Ed.*

WHAT COULD YOU SEE?

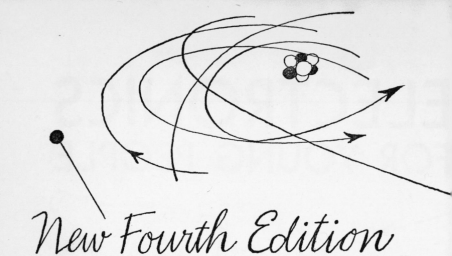

New Fourth Edition

Including Nuclear Energy
Automation
Computers
Miniaturization
and More

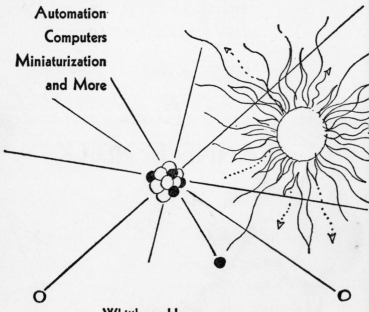

Whittlesey House
McGRAW-HILL BOOK COMPANY, INC.
NEW YORK   TORONTO   LONDON

ELECTRONICS
FOR YOUNG PEOPLE

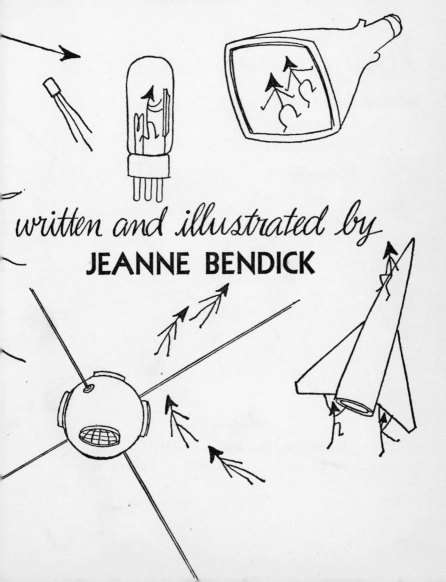

written and illustrated by
JEANNE BENDICK

The author wishes to thank the many people who helped with this book, but most of all Marc Bendick of the Systems Development Company, who checked the complete text and pictures.

621.38

Cop. 1

St. Theodore School
6201 S. PAULINA STREET
CHICAGO 36, ILLINOIS
351

PUBLISHED BY WHITTLESEY HOUSE
A Division of the McGraw-Hill Book Company, Inc.

PRINTED IN THE UNITED STATES OF AMERICA

Contents

C261

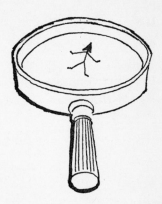

Chapter One
WHAT IS AN ELECTRON?

No MATTER where in the world you look, a part of whatever in the world you see is made mostly of electrons. The air you breathe is electrons (and some other things we'll talk about in a minute). So is the house you live in, the shoes on your feet and the feet in your shoes. You yourself are built of electrons.

You can't see an electron—it is millions of times smaller than the smallest thing you've ever seen. Trillions of electrons wouldn't weigh as much as a feather or be as big as the head of a pin.

The stuff of which everything in the universe is made is called *matter*. Matter is built of electrons (and those other things we'll talk about in a minute), just as a house is built of bricks. Some of this matter we call "live." People and trees, animals and flowers are built of this kind. Some of it does not seem to be alive, like the matter in glass or coins, but all matter is basically alike.

7

What Is an Electron?

Electrons are really tiny, always-moving bits of pure electricity. If you could see them they might look like tiny worlds whirling around a sun, just as our earth and the other planets whirl around our sun in the sky. The sun's gravity holds its planets so securely in place that we can't imagine separating them. It was a long time before men learned how to separate electrons from their sun, which is called a *nucleus*. (If there are more than one, they are called *nuclei*.)

A nucleus is made of charges of electricity too, but they are different from electrons. Every electron is a tiny charge of negative electricity, but in the nucleus there are charges of positive electricity called *protons*. Protons are smaller than electrons, but much heavier. There are other particles in the nucleus called *neutrons* which have no electric charge at all.

Still another kind of particle in the nucleus seems exactly like an electron with a positive charge. Like an electron it has almost no weight. This particle is called a *positron*. It appears only when the nucleus is smashed, then disappears almost instantly. Some scientists think positrons and neutrons together form protons. Others think a positron may be a special kind of energy, created when the nucleus of an atom is smashed.

All the particles in the nucleus cling together, bound by a power that is one of the strongest forces in the world —a million times stronger than the force of gravity.

A nucleus and the electrons whirling around it make up an *atom*. The positive protons in the nucleus of the atom pull very hard on the negative electrons, keeping them

What Is an Electron?

in position, just as the sun's gravity keeps the planets circling it in their positions.

This picture gives you an idea of the way an atom is arranged, but the page of a book isn't big enough to show you how large the orbits of electrons are, compared to the size of the nucleus. If the nucleus were the size of the one on this page, an atom would be a quarter of a mile across.

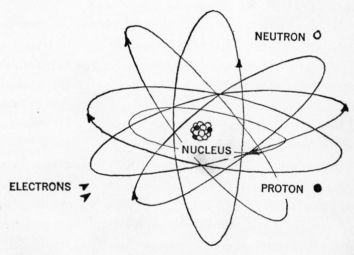

An atom might look like this

Almost all the weight in an atom is in the nucleus. Although a proton is almost a thousand times smaller than an electron, it weighs 1,840 times as much. Even a complicated nucleus with many protons and neutrons is probably smaller than a single electron.

Nuclei and electrons whirling around them make up atoms, and atoms make up all the matter in the world. That is why we say that all matter is basically alike.

What Is an Electron?

If all atoms were exactly alike, there would be only one kind of matter in the world. But some atoms have more protons than others, and more electrons arranged in different ways. There are more than a hundred kinds of atoms and these make up the simplest kind of matter, called the *elements*.

Elements come in many forms and three states. They may be changed from one state to another. Some are gases, some are liquids, some solids. Helium, which is a very light gas, is an element. Iron and gold are elements. The difference between one element and another is the number of electrons, protons, and neutrons in their atoms.

If the atoms of all these elements stayed apart from each other there would be only about a hundred different things in the world. But elements can combine into *compounds*. Hydrogen and oxygen combine to make water. Carbon, hydrogen, and oxygen combine to make sugar. Many elements and compounds combine to make things so unlike as trees and people, seas and stones. Actually, they are all made up of electrons whirling around their nuclei.

Just as electrons and nuclei together build atoms, groups of atoms build *molecules*. A molecule is the smallest particle of matter that can be identified as that particular kind of matter. An atom of the element hydrogen, for example, is made up of only one electron circling its nucleus. As soon as two hydrogen atoms are combined with an atom of the element oxygen, they become a molecule of the familiar compound, water.

The way atoms combine with other atoms is called *valence*.

10

What Is an Electron?

Some atoms will not combine at all. They have no valence. Some will combine with many other atoms. You might think of atoms as holding hands. Some have no hands to hold on to other atoms with. Some have several. But when an atom holds on to other atoms it must use all its hands, leaving none free.

A one-handed atom (we say it has a valence of one) combines like this.

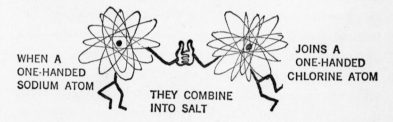

WHEN A ONE-HANDED SODIUM ATOM

THEY COMBINE INTO SALT

JOINS A ONE-HANDED CHLORINE ATOM

Others with more hands combine like this to make molecules.

NO FREE HANDS!

Sometimes it takes a great many atoms to make a molecule, but even molecules are very, very small—some are only about a hundred-millionth of an inch across.

What Is an Electron?

Because molecules themselves are so small, we thought for a long time that the atoms they were made of were the smallest things in the world. Scientists built all sorts of complicated machines for studying atoms. One after another, they came to the conclusion that atoms were made of tiny bits of electricity circling a nucleus. They called these bits of electricity *electrons*.

Electron was not a new word. It had been used for a long time to describe the sparks of electricity that make up a big electric charge like a flash of lightning.

After experimenters made the important discovery that everything was built of these invisible, always-moving charges of electricity, they set about learning to put them to work. The science of making electrons work is *electronics*.

Electrons at work are electronic energy, but there is another kind of energy in an atom that has power of quite a different sort. This is the power released by the exploding nucleus of an atom. It is called *nuclear* or *atomic energy*.

Electronics is the science of the electrons. It is the way we harness them and put them to work doing things men have never been able to do before. Electronics "sees" millions of light years across the universe. It aims and fires rockets into space. It guides planes and ships, diagnoses diseases, translates languages and works out problems. Electronics has become our helper with a thousand hands.

Chapter Two
STARTING
ELECTRONS TO
WORK

IF YOU HAD a team of work horses you would have to harness them before you could put them to work. In the same way, we had to find a way to harness electrons. We had to find a way to make electrons go where they were sent instead of sticking close to their nuclei.

Scientists studied different kinds of matter. They thought that the electrons in some kinds might move around more easily than the electrons in others. They were right. For example, the electrons in metal are fairly free because they are not bound to their nuclei as tightly as the electrons in some other things.

For this reason, metal is a good *conductor* of electric current. The billions of particles of electricity that make up electric current bump each other all along the electric wire. That is why the electric appliances in your house are connected to the wall socket by metal wire.

If you were reading this book under an electric lamp and somebody pulled the wire out of the socket, the light would go out. The electricity has not been turned off, but it has no way to get from the wall socket to the light bulb. It can go only where it is pushed. Generally it cannot travel through the air and get into the light bulb by itself.

The electrons in copper wire carrying electric current don't all come in one end and go out the other like water goes through a garden hose. Electric current comes in from the power plant that supplies your house, and current is pushed out, but the electrons that make up the wire are there all the time. These electrons are always moving around and changing places every which way. Before they can be put to work something has to make many of them go in the same direction. They don't have any power until they push along the wire together.

Electrons in a wire are always doing this but

To have power they must all do this.

When you turn on the electric switch you are forcing the free electrons (electrons that have come apart from their nuclei) to push each other in one direction in

14

a steady stream along the wire to the appliance.

At the wall socket, more and more negative electrons are being pushed into the wire. At the other end of the wire, positive atoms are pulling these electrons toward themselves. (Positive atoms are atoms that have lost electrons and are hungry for more.) This is what makes current flow through a conductor. Electrons are pushed in at one end and pulled toward the other end. The pressure which makes electrons flow from one end of the wire to the other is called *voltage*. The higher the pressure of electrons in a wire, the higher the voltage.

A *volt* is the measurement of the pressure that makes electric current flow. It does not take many volts to run your radio, but a tremendous number of volts is needed in an electric railroad system. You have probably noticed signs along a railroad track, fastened to the towers that hold the overhead electric wires. The signs may say, "DANGER. 16,000 VOLTS." That is the amount of electric pressure running through those wires.

The power plant where this pressure is made may be hundreds of miles away from the railroad track and from the wall socket in your house. The real beginning of this electric power may be even farther away than the power plant—in a coal mine or an oil well or a great river. Water power or coal or oil or even atomic fuel works the generator in the power plant. The generator makes electricity and sends it through wires and cables, across the countryside and under the streets to your house. Then, when you turn on your electric switch, this voltage pushes electrons up the wire to their job.

Starting Electrons to Work

Here is an experiment that may give you a better idea of how pressure turns the electrons in the wire into electric power.

Put some tiny pebbles or beads into a large drinking straw. If you hold it level they may move around a little in the straw or even trickle out, but they will just drop to the ground. Now hold a piece of paper in front of the straw and blow hard into the other end. The pebbles will shoot out of the straw so fast that they will knock the paper aside. Some may even tear right through it.

By applying pressure you have forced the pebbles to rush through the straw and have even given them enough power to push away the paper. In the same way, the pressure of voltage, applied to electrons in a wire, will make

Voltage is pushing the electrons through the wire.

them shoot through it in a current. If the voltage is strong enough, the electrons will jump right out of it just as the pebbles shot out of the straw.

In electronics, pushing electrons out of their metal is the first step in starting them to work. But if you pushed them out into the air, they would be like wild horses, scattering in every direction. Before you can catch electrons to harness them you must fence them in. The enclosure you use is called an *electron tube*.

Starting Electrons to Work

Most electron tubes are vacuums. An electric light bulb is a vacuum, and so is a radio tube. This means that as much air as possible has been taken out of them. (Some electron tubes do contain small amounts of gas.)

There are two reasons for removing the air from electron tubes. First, air molecules are so big, compared to electrons, that the electrons would smack into them and

come to a stop. The other is that the oxygen in air makes things burn when they get hot. If there is no air, the metal parts of a tube cannot burn, no matter how hot they get.

If you look at an electric light bulb you will see a thin wire, either looped or zigzagging through the middle. This wire is called a *filament,* and it is made of a metal called tungsten. When electric current runs into the filament it starts pushing and jiggling the electrons there, bumping them into each other until they move faster and faster.

Even molecules of ordinary air move fast—about 500 yards a second. When they are heated they move much faster. As the atoms in the filament speed up, they start sending off little rays of energy.

Starting Electrons to Work

The same thing happens when you make a fire by rubbing two pieces of wood together. It is called *friction*. When you rub the sticks together, the atoms in the wood jiggle against each other, sending off the heat rays that start the fire. The electrons in the filament of a light bulb can't start a fire because there is no air in the bulb, and nothing can burn without air.

You can prove this by putting a glass over a lighted candle. As soon as the flame has used up all the air under the glass, it will go out.

The filament can't burn
because there is no air

The candle goes out
when the air is used up

The electrons in the hot filament send off the white-hot glow we call electric light. If the light bulb were not a vacuum, the filament would soon burn up and the light would go out. Sometimes the atoms move so fast that they jump right out of the filament. Then they stop working to make light, and are just dark smudges inside the glass bulb.

18

Starting Electrons to Work

A radio tube is different from a light bulb. Here, as in all electron tubes, the electrons are *supposed* to leave the filament and they don't start work until they are free. Different kinds of electron tubes get the electrons loose in different ways, but getting them loose is the first thing they must all do before the electrons can be put to work.

This is the big difference between things that are run electrically and things that are run electronically. When electricity is used as power, the electric current never leaves the wires that conduct it. Some of the electrons that make up electric current are free in the spaces between the atoms, but some stay with their nuclei. These atoms try to hold on to the free electrons that flow along the wire, and the free electrons have a hard time getting past. Sometimes they are pulled into the atoms, and other electrons are pushed out. Part of their energy is wasted because of this tug o' war that is always going on. It is used up in just getting through the wire.

As free electrons flow through a wire, they have to push their way past the atoms in the wire.

The struggle by the atoms in the wire to keep the free electrons from getting past is called *resistance*. The harder it is for electrons to get through the wire, the more resistance the wire has and the more voltage it takes to push

19

them through. A copper wire has less resistance than a tungsten wire. That is why electric current flows through the copper wire. In the tungsten wire the battle is so much fiercer that all the pushing and shoving makes the wire glow with heat.

When things are run electronically, the electric current that has been imprisoned in the wire is freed. Free electrons have more power and are easier to control than electrons that are always being pulled here and there by their nuclei. The job of electronics is to get these electrons loose and make them use their energy to do a special sort of work.

Chapter Three
ELECTRON
TUBES

THE BEGINNING of electronics is in the vacuum tubes where electrons are freed. Some of these tubes are no bigger than marbles, and some are 25 feet tall, but certain things about all of them are alike.

They all contain metal as the *source* of the electrons, the place from which they come. In a radio tube the source is called a filament, as it is in a light bulb. In most electron tubes the source is a *cathode*. A filament is a thin wire that is heated itself. A cathode has a separate heater.

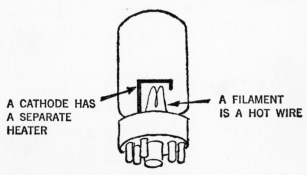

A CATHODE HAS
A SEPARATE
HEATER

A FILAMENT
IS A HOT WIRE

Electron Tubes

The shell of the tube is called the *envelope*. The envelope must be airtight so nothing will burn. There must be a way for the electric current to get in. And after the tube has changed the current in some way, there must be a place for it to get out.

All electron tubes have a *plate* to collect the electrons once they are free. This plate is usually called the *anode*. To understand the way the anode is used, we have to understand another very important thing about electrons and atoms.

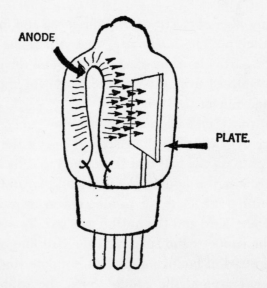

In the first chapter we said that the charges of electricity in the nucleus were different from electrons. Electrons are bits of negative electricity, but in the nucleus are bits of positive electricity called protons.

22

Electron Tubes

It is a law of nature that a positive electric charge always pulls a negative charge toward it and the negative electricity has to go. That is why electrons stay close to their nuclei—they are negative, and the positive protons are pulling on them. And that is the reason for the anode in an electron tube.

Electrons are always flowing out of the anode, which leaves the nuclei there positive and hungry for more electrons. As soon as electrons are freed from the cathode, they are yanked by these hungry positive nuclei toward the anode.

The number of electrons, and the speed and force with which they hit the anode, are what makes the kind of current a particular tube hands on. But first the electrons have to be freed from their source by getting them apart from their nuclei.

Have you ever had a ball-and-paddle game? Imagine the nucleus pulling on the electrons just as the wooden paddle pulls on the ball that is attached to it by a rubber band. Usually you bounce the ball, and the rubber band keeps pulling it back to the paddle. If you keep bouncing the ball very hard and fast until it gets farther and farther away, the rubber band snaps and the ball flies off.

But instead of bouncing the ball, suppose you whirled it very fast *around* the paddle. Soon the rubber band would stretch way out, and the ball would make a great circle around you. The faster it went, the more the rubber band would stretch. When all the stretch was gone, it would break.

23

Electron Tubes

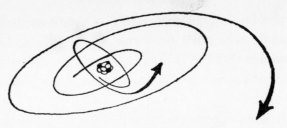

The faster the electrons whirl, the farther they get from their nuclei.

Electrons are freed in the same way. They are forced at high speed farther and farther away from their nucleus until the imaginary rubber band breaks and off they go.

To free electrons, something has to make them whirl fast enough to break away from their nuclei. In most electron tubes, that something is *heat*.

Heat speeds up the movement of electrons and makes them come apart from their nuclei more easily. That is just what you do when you melt something by heating it. The electrons in melted chocolate, for example, are much less tightly bound together than the electrons in a chocolate bar.

Electric current heats the cathode until the electrons in it whirl fast enough to break away. As soon as they are free, the strong, positive electricity in the anode starts pulling on them, and they fly across the tube and crash into it.

In between the filament or cathode and the anode, there is usually a way to control the electrons.

Sometimes the controlling is done by the electrons themselves. When too many jump out of the cathode for the anode to handle, they crowd together in a sort of

Electron Tubes

screen around the cathode. The electrons that leave the cathode now can't get through this screen. There is no place for them to go but back into the cathode until the electrons forming the screen have been pulled away to the plate.

In some electron tubes a real screen is put between the cathode and the anode to control the electrons. This screen is called the *grid*.

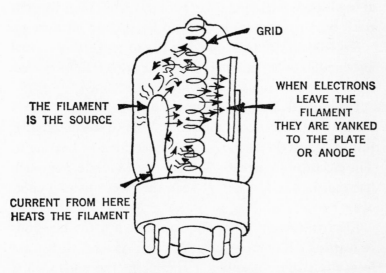

GRID

THE FILAMENT
IS THE SOURCE

WHEN ELECTRONS
LEAVE THE
FILAMENT
THEY ARE YANKED
TO THE PLATE
OR ANODE

CURRENT FROM HERE
HEATS THE FILAMENT

A radio tube works like this

The grid works like a venetian blind. When it is fully open the electrons all sail through, just as lots of sun comes into a room if the slats of the venetian blind are open. As you close the shutters of the blind, less and less sun gets through. As the openings of the grid are closed in an electron tube, fewer and fewer electrons get through.

25

Electron Tubes

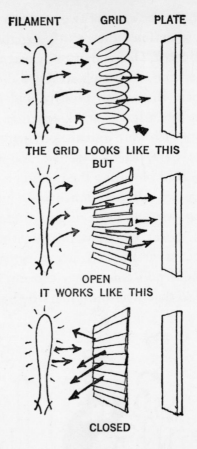

FILAMENT   GRID   PLATE

THE GRID LOOKS LIKE THIS

BUT

OPEN

IT WORKS LIKE THIS

CLOSED

The grid in an electron tube may look like a screen, or a spiral of fine wire, or a sheet of metal punched full of holes. It really has nothing mechanical that opens or closes. What happens is this: A separate current of electricity runs into the screen. As this current is made up of negative electrons, the free electrons in the tube jump back away from it. We say the negative electricity in the grid *repels* the negative electrons.

26

Electron Tubes

If you ever put the ends of two magnets together, you noticed that sometimes they stuck together and sometimes they fell apart. One end of every magnet is different from the other end. Although it is not the same thing, we can compare them with positive and negative electricity. When the magnets stuck together the different ends or *poles* of each were touching. When they fell apart the like poles were placed together and they repelled each other. Instead of calling the poles of a magnet negative or positive, we call them north and south.

In a similar way, as more negative electricity flows into the grid, fewer electrons can get through to the plate. The grid is closing as if it had actual shutters. It is a sort of traffic policeman for electrons, stopping and starting them so that electron traffic won't get all snarled up.

There are other ways of controlling electrons between the cathode and the anode. Sometimes a shield over the cathode concentrates the electrons into a beam, which is

Electron Tubes

made to swing one way or the other by applying current, or by magnets. But the grid is more usual.

The vacuum tube with a hot cathode and a grid for controlling electrons is probably the most common type of electron tube. Radio tubes are this kind.

Another kind of tube uses the cathode and the anode differently. The anode has a tremendous positive charge that yanks the electrons right away from the hot cathode. Not only are the electrons boiled out of the cathode and yanked by the anode, but they are aimed and shot through a sort of gun in between. The electrons crash into the anode with such speed and force that they almost knock the atoms there apart. While these shaken atoms are trying to settle down again, they give off the powerful rays we call *X-rays*. This tube is an X-ray tube.

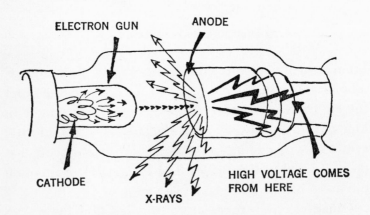

The harder electrons crash into the anode, the shorter and more powerful are the X-rays that are sent out. Tubes designed to make X-rays that go through steel might be powered by a million volts. Medical X-rays need much less.

In some electron tubes the source of electrons is a curved sheet of metal or a special coating on the tube that reacts to light the way other cathodes react to heat. A

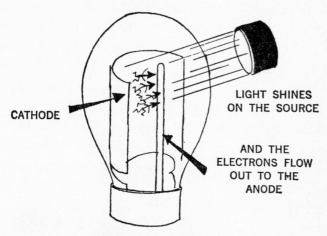

CATHODE

LIGHT SHINES
ON THE SOURCE

AND THE
ELECTRONS FLOW
OUT TO THE
ANODE

An electric eye works like this.

beam of light is used to chase electrons out of the source. The brighter the light shining on the cathode, the faster the electrons in it move and the more jump out. This kind of tube is called a *phototube* or *electric eye*. Electric eyes work magic fountains, burglar alarms and doors that open and shut by themselves. The sound track of a motion picture is run by an electric eye too.

Other electron tubes have very small amounts of special kinds of gas. When electrons jump out of the heated filament they bump into the gas atoms in the tube and knock some electrons out of them.

Electron Tubes

When an atom either gains or loses an electron we say that it becomes *ionized,* and the atoms are called *ions.* The ions that are minus an electron are positive, so they start away from the positive anode, back toward the negative cathode. These ions form a positive bridge for

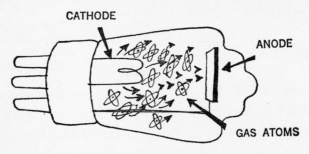

A gas tube works like this.

electrons to cross on. As new electrons jump out of the cathode they fill in the spaces in the gas atoms, but more electrons are bumped out. The electrons from the gas atoms and the electrons from the cathode flow together in a strong current to the plate. These tubes are used in factories where great amounts of power are needed. Gas electron tubes are used to make aluminum for pots and pans and airplanes. Fluorescent lights are gas-filled tubes too.

A kind of electron tube called a *magnetron* uses magnetism to control the flow of electrons. The filament of this tube runs through a metal cylinder which is the plate. When the filament is heated, electrons fly off to the plate. But if a magnetic charge is applied, it makes the electrons change their path and fly in a curve, instead of directly to the plate. The more powerful the magnetism,

Electron Tubes

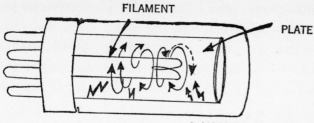

FILAMENT

PLATE

A magnetron works like this

A MAGNET ON THE OUTSIDE
OF THE TUBE SUPPLIES THE
CHARGE TO MAKE THE
ELECTRONS FLY IN A CURVE

the more curved the path of the electrons becomes. If they make a complete curve they never reach the plate at all, but return to the filament. Then, no current passes through the tube. Very small changes in magnetism make a big difference in the amount of current flowing.

Magnetrons were especially developed to handle very short-wave radio signals and are an important part of radar equipment. The big brother of the magnetron, the *amplitron,* generates many times as much energy as the magnetron does, but it works in the same way.

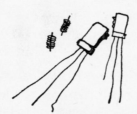

NOT REALLY TUBES

A *transistor* isn't really an electron tube, but in many cases it does exactly the same job. In some kinds of electronic equipment transistors have taken the place of amplifying tubes. Transistors are made of special metals

31

—usually germanium or silicon. They have several advantages over electron tubes.

Transistors are tiny—sometimes no bigger than a match head. They have replaced the tubes in very small radios, in hearing aids and Geiger counters, in portable television receivers and many kinds of computers.

THE TRANSISTOR IS MUCH SMALLER THAN A SMALL ELECTRON TUBE

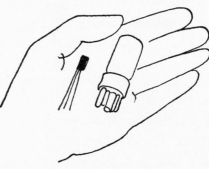

A transistor does not need much power. The flashlight-sized batteries in a portable radio are quite strong enough.

Transistors do not have to produce heat to free electrons so they do not get as hot as tubes do.

Because a transistor is just a bit of metal and wire, it is not as delicate as a tube.

The parts of a transistor have different names than the parts of an electron tube, but they do the same kinds of jobs.

The *emitter* is like the cathode, giving off electrons. This is because something is added to the metal in the emitter, making it negative.

The *collector* is like the plate, attracting electrons. Other elements are combined with the metal in the collector, making it positive.

Electron Tubes

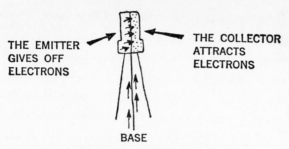

THE EMITTER GIVES OFF ELECTRONS

THE COLLECTOR ATTRACTS ELECTRONS

BASE

CURRENT COMES IN FROM THE BATTERY

A transistor works like this

The *base* is like the grid. Current comes into the base from the battery.

A kind of improvement on the transistor is called a *spacistor*. It can be made of any one of a number of materials, and it can operate at temperatures that would melt a transistor.

The *cryotron* is an electronic device that may some day replace electron tubes, transistors and spacistors. It looks like a tiny electromagnet and is so small that a hundred of them would fit easily into a teaspoon. A cryotron is made of coils of wire as thin as a spider's web, wound around a straight bit of wire. It will make *really* tiny electronic devices possible. Engineers are always working to perfect smaller practical equipment. This is called *miniaturization*.

Later we're going to talk about the astonishing things these tubes and other devices do every day. The most complicated jobs are usually performed by a combination of several kinds of tubes, often working with transistors.

33

Chapter Four
THE BEGINNINGS OF ELECTRONICS— 2,600 YEARS OF ELECTRICITY

NOBODY sat down and thought out the science of electronics all at once. For hundreds of years men have been discovering, sometimes by accident but usually through long and careful experiments, little bits of information. Then they pieced these together with things other men had discovered. Any of the sciences as we know them today is built of thousands of discoveries by thousands of people. Many of them never saw each other. Many of them lived at different times.

When these bits of information are fitted together like pieces of a giant jigsaw puzzle, a picture begins to form. Before the study of any subject can be called a science, the picture must be fairly complete. Sometimes there are parts that don't seem to fit anywhere and have to be put aside until there are new places to try them out.

In most sciences the puzzle is never finished. It keeps getting bigger and more details are added all the time. Sometimes no one will add to the puzzle for years. Sometimes the pieces will fit into place quickly. Sometimes two people, working entirely apart from one another will both pounce upon the right piece at the same time. Often a new piece will show that the puzzle is much bigger than anyone thought.

The first piece in the puzzle of electronics was laid down almost 2,600 years ago. Nebuchadnezzar was king of Babylon. The Japanese Empire had just been founded, and Buddha was about to be born. This first piece was a clear, yellow-brown stone (which is really petrified tree sap), washed up out of the sea. We know this stone as amber. The Greeks called it *elektron*.

Thales, a wise man of Greece, studied the amber carefully, and made an interesting discovery. If he rubbed it very hard it attracted bits of straw or feathers, or sometimes lint from his robes.

Thales had made a study of another kind of stone that was common in Greece. It was called the magnes stone. The Greeks thought it was magic because it could attract and hold bits of iron. Today we call this stone a loadstone or *magnet*.

Thales studied the attraction the magnet had for iron and the attraction the rubbed amber had for straw and feathers and decided they were the same thing. Here Thales made a mistake. (He didn't make many errors. He was the first man to predict an eclipse of the sun and he thought out a good deal of the geometry that is taught in school today.)

But when he decided that elektron and the magic iron were alike, he fitted the first two pieces of the puzzle together wrong. He did it so well, and they *looked* so right together that it was more than two thousand years later, in 1600, that anyone discovered his mistake.

In 1600 new worlds were opening in all directions. Elizabeth I was Queen of England, and the first colonists were coming to America. The power of Spain was fading and the power of England was rising. In 1600 William Gilbert, physician to Queen Elizabeth, wrote a book called *On the Magnet.*

Gilbert discovered some important things that we all take for granted today. One of them was that the earth itself is a giant magnet with two poles, just like those of a toy magnet. Another was that some things have the power to *generate* or produce electricity when they are rubbed. We generate all the electricity we use today.

You can generate electricity yourself by rubbing a glass rod or a comb hard with a piece of silk. You are applying friction and in a minute or so you will feel the comb getting hot where you are rubbing it. Now, if you hold the comb over some bits of paper, they will be attracted to it just as pins are to a magnet. Later on we'll talk about *why* the comb attracts those bits of paper, but you have generated electricity and put it to work.

But you had to *do* something to the comb to make it attract other things, while a true magnet will attract them by itself, without any help from you.

Gilbert was the first to notice this difference. He called the things in which he could generate electricity "electrics," after the Greek word for amber. And he called the power to work which was created "electric force."

Gilbert fitted some important parts into the puzzle, but there were some he could not find. He tested metal and when he found that it would not generate electricity he called it a "nonelectric." He never discovered that electricity moved freely through metal. In fact he thought it did not move at all, but was always still, or *static*.

Thales had thought that an electric force and a magnetic force were the same thing. Gilbert decided that they were entirely different and separate. We know now that it is not possible to have one without the other. All electric current creates a magnetic force, an area around it that has the same kind of power a real magnet has.

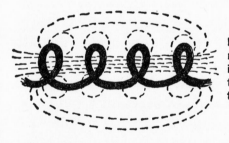

If electric current were running through this coil of wire, it would create a magnetic force around it something like this.

This magnetic area around an electric current is called a *magnetic field*. There is a magnetic field around every electric wire and power line. There is a magnetic field around every magnet, even around the earth itself. A magnetic field can be used to generate electricity. Why this is so is still one of the missing pieces of the puzzle.

37

Beginnings of Electronics—2,600 Years of Electricity

The first machine that generated electricity was built in Germany by Otto von Guericke in 1663, the year before New Amsterdam became New York.

Von Guericke's generator was a big sulphur ball with a long iron handle. When he revolved the ball and rubbed his hand against it, sparks of electricity flew out of the ball.

Scientists worked hard at many queer inventions, trying to generate electricity. One made himself a big paddle wheel, and tipped the paddles with amber. Then he fastened his cat under the wheel. Every time the wheel turned, the paddles stroked the cat's back and sparks of electricity flew out of his fur. The machine was generating electricity but it wasn't very practical.

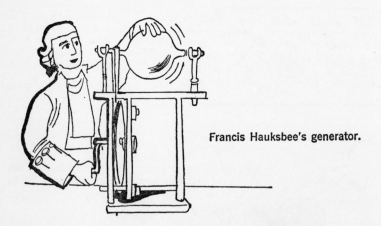

Francis Hauksbee's generator.

In 1709, Francis Hauksbee built what might be called the first electric light. It was a globe on a handle like von Guericke's, but Hauksbee's globe was made of glass. When he held his hand against the turning globe, sparks of electricity filled it. Hauksbee could read very large print by the light from that globe.

In 1729 an Englishman named Stephen Gray put the next piece into the puzzle. He proved that some materials, like the metals Gilbert had called nonelectrics, were good conductors of electricity and that others (most of Gilbert's "electrics") were poor conductors.

We said before that a good conductor was one in which electrons can move freely from one point to another because they are not bound tightly to their nuclei. Can you guess why electricity does not move freely through a poor conductor? The electrons are so tightly bound to their nuclei that they have a hard time breaking loose. Poor conductors are called *insulators*. The electric wires in

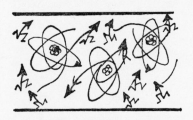

Electrons can move freely through a good conductor.

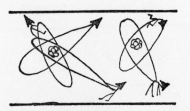

In a poor conductor, electrons are too tightly bound to their nuclei to move around freely.

your house are insulated with poor conductors like rubber or silk. This keeps you from getting a shock when you touch a wire.

Beginnings of Electronics—2,600 Years of Electricity

In 1733 a Frenchman, Du Fay, discovered what makes electricity move through a conductor. He decided that there were two entirely different kinds of electricity, and that the unlike kinds attracted each other while the like kinds repelled each other, or jumped apart.

We know now that what Du Fay thought was a different kind of electricity was really atoms that had lost some of their electrons.

This pull of positive atoms on negative electrons had been confusing scientists into thinking that electricity and magnetism were the same thing. It looked like the pull of a magnet.

In America in the years before the Revolution, Benjamin Franklin did a lot of work on the puzzle. He experimented with negative and positive charges of electricity and discovered that they could attract each other across space, without being connected by a conductor.

Some of Franklin's ideas about electricity are still accepted today, two hundred years later. One idea is that all electricity is made up of tiny charges which he called particles and we call electrons.

Another idea is that electricity is neither made nor destroyed. There is the same amount of electricity in the universe now that there was at the beginning of time.

Beginnings of Electronics—2,600 Years of Electricity

When this electricity is made to move in one direction it has power, and becomes electric current. All electricity is *energy,* and energy is the ability to do work.

Franklin proved, too, with his famous kite experiment that lightning is just a giant discharge of electricity and no different from any other kind of electricity. He proved that we can direct this charge, and make it go where we want it to.

In 1780, while the American Revolution was being fought, an Italian professor named Luigi Galvani was dissecting a frog to study. The legs of the frog were hung on copper hooks. When he touched a nerve in the dead frog's legs with his steel knife, they jerked. Neither Galvani nor the frog knew it, but in a way those legs contained the first electric battery. They proved that electricity could be stored.

Until then, nobody had ever made electricity *do* anything. When Galvani touched his steel knife to the nerve, electric current flowed through the leg to the copper wire in the muscle, and the muscle jerked.

Alessandro Volta repeated Galvani's experiment with the frog's leg and decided it wasn't anything special about the frog's leg itself that made the current. It must be the two different kinds of metal connected by the moist conductor of the frog's leg.

Volta made a pile of disks of copper and zinc, separated by cloth that had been soaked in salt water. When he touched both ends at once he got a sharp shock. When he connected the ends there was a spark. Volta had built the first battery and generated the first electric current

41

in modern times. (Archaeologists have dug up electric batteries that were used thousands of years ago in the Middle East.) Volta made his battery in 1800.

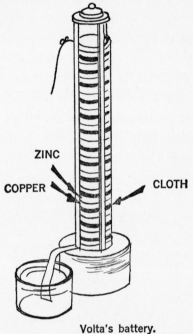

ZINC

COPPER

CLOTH

Volta's battery.

Twenty years later a Danish scientist, Hans Christian Oersted, came back to the confusing problem of magnetic and electric force. Oersted proved that all electricity creates a magnetic field around it that can be used to make more electricity. And right after Oersted's discovery, André Ampère said that a magnet *is* a magnet because little currents of electricity are always moving around the molecules that make up a magnet.

42

Beginnings of Electronics—2,600 Years of Electricity

Now the pieces began to fall into place faster and faster. Scientists all over the world were discovering new things about electricity, and finding ways to put it to work.

In 1883 the Panama Canal had just been started, and inventors were working on the first horseless carriages. In 1883 Thomas Edison was experimenting with his new invention, the electric light bulb. He was trying to find out what made the filament burn up so quickly. One day Edison sealed a metal plate into the bulb and connected the plate to the positive pole of a separate battery. (One terminal or pole of a battery is positive, one is negative.)

Although they were not connected, current flowed across the bulb from the filament to the plate. Edison was puzzled, but he finally decided that the current couldn't

Edison made this first electronic tube without knowing it. He did not realize that current flowed from the filament to the plate.

be flowing across the tube from the filament, but must be coming into the plate from the battery.

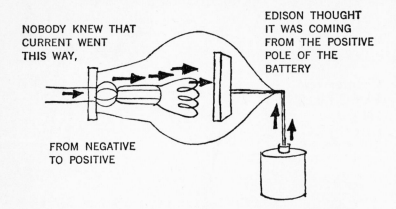

NOBODY KNEW THAT
CURRENT WENT
THIS WAY,

EDISON THOUGHT
IT WAS COMING
FROM THE POSITIVE
POLE OF THE
BATTERY

FROM NEGATIVE
TO POSITIVE

Everybody believed then that current always flowed from the positive to the negative. Current in an electron tube flows from the negative to the positive, but scientists then did not know anything about electrons or how they behaved. Edison invented the first electron tube without knowing it.

Electricity was growing up after 2,600 years.

Chapter Five
ELECTRICITY
INTO
ELECTRONICS—
50 YEARS

A<small>T THE END</small> of the last century a few men, working separately, laid the foundation of all the things we know about electrons today.

One of these men was Hendrik Antoon Lorentz, a Dutchman. Lorentz started by imagining that all space between the atoms of air was filled with something he called the *ether*. Through it, little particles of electricity moved constantly, making the ether around them electric. Lorentz said these particles of electricity were all the same, whether they were in space or in something that looks as solid as you do. He said that all the solid things in the world were mostly space anyhow, peppered with these tiny atoms of electricity. When the atoms were closer together, the matter was *dense,* like gold. When they were farther apart they were less dense, like gas.

If all the space in you were taken out and just the particles of electricity that form matter were left, you would be no bigger than a vitamin pill.

One reason things *seem* solid is that electrons move so fast in their orbits that they fill them. Have you ever made a fast circle in the air with a lighted flash light? You *know* there is only one point of light, but it looks like a solid ring.

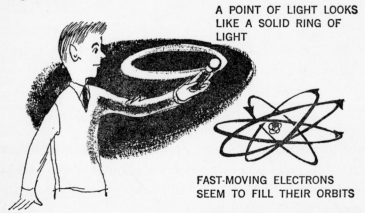

A POINT OF LIGHT LOOKS LIKE A SOLID RING OF LIGHT

FAST-MOVING ELECTRONS SEEM TO FILL THEIR ORBITS

In 1897, J. J. Thomson, an Englishman, said that atoms could not possibly be the smallest particles of matter. If they were, how could you explain the great force that kept them in place? How could you explain the power of some electricity to attract other electricity or to repel it?

Thomson decided that there must be at least two kinds of electricity in every atom, and if there were two kinds of anything in it, an atom itself could not be the smallest particle of matter.

We know now that there is only one way an atom can be made. It must have a nucleus of positive electricity that keeps particles of negative electricity moving around it. This helps to explain what keeps the atoms themselves in place. The negative electrons are held there by the posi-

46

tive nucleus. They are also held there because they are nearer to the negative electrons of other atoms than they

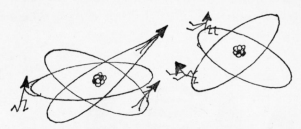

Negative electrons are held in place because they are pulled toward their own positive nucleus and pushed away from other atoms by the electrons of those atoms.

are to the positive nuclei of those atoms. Those other electrons repel them. But nobody is sure yet what keeps electrons whirling around their nucleus at a distance instead of being pulled into it.

It is easier for an electron to stay where it is than to go whirling out of its atom. But if it should leave, that atom would be unbalanced. Usually every atom, whether it has one or eighty electrons, tries to keep an exactly equal balance of positive and negative electricity. No matter how disturbed it is, every atom tries as hard as possible to keep that balance. An atom that becomes unbalanced because it has lost an electron will try desperately to yank one out of another atom to take its place.

The experiment with the comb and the piece of silk is a good example of this. When you rubbed the comb hard, you whirled some of its electrons off onto the silk. Then when you held the comb close to the bits of paper they were attracted to the comb because the positive atoms in the comb were trying to grab back some of the electrons they lost onto the silk. Those positive atoms were pulling so hard on the electrons in the bits of paper that the paper itself stuck to the comb. Don't forget that the atoms in the paper were trying to hold on to those electrons too. If you could stand in the middle of a field and pull a barn toward you, just by drawing in your breath, you would not be pulling harder than the electrons in the comb pulled on the paper.

When you think about the incredible smallness of the particles of positive electricity that pulled the scraps of paper toward them, you can begin to see how powerful the forces in an atom are. The force in the nucleus itself is the strongest thing in the world. When this force is released, it is atomic energy.

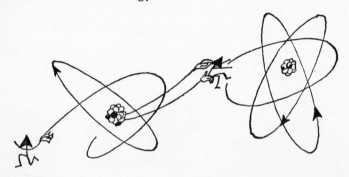

Every atom will try to steal electrons to take the place of any it loses.

The whole science of electronics is built upon the discovery that a positive atom will try to pull toward itself enough negative electrons to balance it. If the nuclei were not always pulling on their electrons, everything in the world would fly to pieces.

48

Electricity Into Electronics—50 Years

Thomson never saw an electron. No one has even seen an atom, and an electron to an atom is like a green pea to a grocery store. But scientists realized that his theories must be true. Here was the greatest source of energy in the world, if they could only find a way to harness it.

In 1883, almost fifteen years earlier, Edison had found a way to harness electrons, but neither he nor anyone else realized it. You remember he had sealed a positively charged metal plate into a vacuum bulb along with a hot filament. This is the basis of all electron tubes today. But for twenty years the *Edison effect,* as the current of free electrons across a vacuum tube is called, lay idle.

In 1904 Sir John Ambrose Fleming rediscovered the Edison effect. He built the first working electron tube. The tube was called the Fleming valve and it was used to pick up radio signals.

All valves control whatever is flowing through the conductor, whether it is water through a water pipe or electrons through a wire. All electron tubes are valves in

Valves are control points.

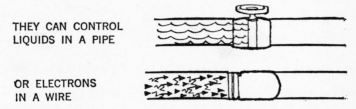

THEY CAN CONTROL
LIQUIDS IN A PIPE

OR ELECTRONS
IN A WIRE

which the electrons are controlled until they reach the wire going out of the tube. Then they are ordinary electric current again. The tube simply interrupts the flow

49

of electrons through a wire and makes them behave in one of several special ways.

The Fleming valve was an electron tube with just a filament and a plate, but in that tube radio signals were changed into direct electric current that could be amplified millions of times.

To *amplify* means to increase or enlarge, and that is the job of many electron tubes. They amplify sound you cannot hear, light you cannot see and electricity that is too weak to work. They build these unhearable, invisible things into sound and light and power.

In 1906, an American, Dr. Lee De Forest, added the third important part to the tube, the grid that controls electrons between the source and the plate.

| Fleming's valve had just a filament and a plate. | De Forest added a grid to control the electrons. | Langmuir added an extra control by making the tube a high-vacuum. |

Now the electron tube was ready and working at several jobs, but it only worked well when the voltage was small.

As the voltage was increased, the electrons got harder to handle. At this point Dr. Irving Langmuir had the idea of removing more air from the tube than anyone had ever done before. (It is just about impossible to get *all* the air out of anything.) When the tube became a *high-vacuum* tube the electrons behaved much better. Without the air atoms to disturb them they were even their own traffic policemen and wouldn't allow more traffic than the plate could handle.

After that, electron tubes worked at much higher voltages. Now the electrons in the tube were ready to go to work amplifying the power of other electrons pushing through wires and of still others that had never been harnessed at all.

Chapter Six
WAVES

THERE IS ENERGY around us all the time, whether we are aware of it or not. Electrons moving in their atoms give off energy. The light, heat and sound that is all around us is energy. All of this energy travels in a kind of motion called waves.

Many scientists believe that electrons in their atoms do not revolve in orbits at all, but behave like trains of waves, reverberating back and forth within the limits of their atoms like echoes in a cave.

There are still many things we do not know about these waves of energy, even though we can direct and control them.

Some of these waves we can see, hear, feel and use by ourselves. Some of them must be amplified by electrons working in tubes before they can be used. These waves are the energy of countless billions of electrons in motion.

There are some things we can learn about all waves from the familiar waves in water. Suppose you fill your bathtub now, and experiment.

If you drop any small object into the tub, it will start ripples that are really small, shallow waves. They will travel away from the object you dropped, in wider and wider circles until they reach the walls of the tub. All waves are started this way. They *radiate* out from a disturbance in these widening circles. If you could see sound waves and light and heat and radio waves, they would make a pattern similar to the ripples in the bathtub. You see those ripples only on the surface of the water, but sound and light and heat waves extend in every direction, like a balloon being blown bigger and bigger.

When the ripples reach the outside of the tub, they hit the wall and start back toward the center again. The

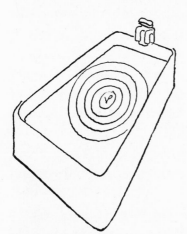

Waves radiate out from a disturbance.

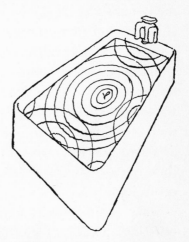

When waves hit an obstacle, they are reflected.

waves are being *reflected* from the walls of the tub. Sound, light, heat and radio waves are reflected too. When a sound wave is reflected we call it an echo. If you look at a white building on a sunny day the reflection of the light waves is dazzling. If you come near the building you can feel the reflection of the sun's heat. If radio waves were not reflected there would be no such thing as radar, or short-wave broadcasting.

Waves

Now turn on the tub faucet so the water falls in slow drops, making even ripples. Hold a pencil in the path of one of these ripples and the little wave will bend around the pencil and go off in a new direction. We say the wave is *deflected,* which means that it has been bent or turned aside.

The small object you dropped, or those drops of water falling into the tub made a disturbance that started the waves. The molecules of water where they fell were shaken out of place and they whirled away from the disturbance, bumping into the molecules next to them, which in turn bumped into the molecules next to *them* and so made the widening ripples. It looks as if the water itself is moving away from the disturbance, but this is not true. The water is staying in the same place and the disturbance is moving through it.

Waves travel THROUGH a medium.

Drop a paper match near the faucet where the ripples are fairly strong. You will notice that although the match may bob up and down on the ripples, or even move in little circles, it stays pretty much in the same place. If the water on which the match is floating were moving, the match would be carried out to the edge of the tub. The waves are passing through the water but they are not taking the water with them. Part of the water will move as the waves disturb it, but after the waves have passed it returns to its original place.

The fact that waves pass through something without taking it with them is even easier to see with a thin piece of rope. Tie one end of the rope to the back of a chair or wedge it into a bureau drawer. Now hold the other end and move it up and down quickly. The rope will form into waves that travel to the fastened end and are then reflected back along the rope. You know that the rope itself is not moving away from you; one end is fastened and you are holding the other. The waves must be traveling through the rope.

Now let's look at the ripples in the bathtub again. The space between the ripples, from the top or *crest* of one to the top of the next one, is the *wave length*. (Waves can also be measured from the bottom or *trough* of one to the trough of the next. From the top of the crest to the bottom of the trough is the *amplitude* of the wave.) All waves are measured in wave lengths. There are tremendous differences in the lengths of some of the waves we can neither see nor hear. Some are thousands of miles long, and some are so short that it takes millions of them to make an inch.

Frequency is the number of waves that form and move away from the disturbance in a second, so the shorter the waves are, the higher their frequency. Instead of saying that waves move, we say they *vibrate*. One complete vibration is called a *cycle*.

When you hear an announcement that a certain radio

Waves

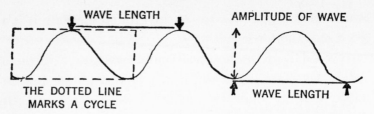

If these three waves vibrated in a second, three would be their frequency.

station operates on a frequency of so many kilocycles, it means that the station sends out radio waves that vibrate that many thousand times a second. Radio waves vibrate so fast that they are measured in thousands or millions. "Kilo" means thousand and "mega" means million.

Waves in water must have the water to move through. If the water were not there the waves could not get from the spot under the faucet where the drop fell to the outside of the tub. If that first drop fell in the empty tub, it could not send a wave to the outside of the tub because there would be nothing through which the wave could travel. We say the water is the *medium* of that particular kind of wave.

The word medium, as we are using it here, means any substance through which waves can travel to get somewhere else. The waves you made in the bathtub could not go anywhere if the water were not there, because water is their medium. A medium is a kind of conductor.

Sound waves must have a medium too. Sound waves can use air as their medium, or water or solid things like steel or the earth. Sometimes you can hear quite distant

56

sounds if you put your ear to the ground, because it is a good medium for sound waves.

If you'd like to see how well sound waves travel through solids, lay your watch down at one end of the longest table in your house. Cover one of your ears with your hand and press the other ear flat against the table, at the opposite end from the watch. You will hear it ticking distinctly, right underneath your ear. The sound waves are traveling through the solid table to you. The table is their medium.

Like waves in water, sound waves must have a medium to get them from one place to another. They cannot travel in a vacuum.

Light, heat and radio waves are different. They do not need a medium. Light, heat and radio waves are called *electromagnetic* waves. Scientists are still not sure what these electromagnetic waves are. They are not electric current, but they seem to be moving electricity. They behave like electrons but they don't appear to have any mass, or solid form.

The greatest source of electromagnetic waves, or radiant energy as it is often called, is the sun. The sun provided light and heat for the earth long before we learned to make these things for ourselves. The light and heat we make are copies of sun power.

Radiations from the sun are started in the same way any waves are—by a disturbance. The tremendous heat of the sun causes its gases to whirl violently in all directions. This terrific heat sends countless electromagnetic waves shooting out into space, just as a heated filament sends electrons shooting out into a vacuum tube.

Radiations from the sun have millions of different wave lengths. Most of them never reach the earth at all. Those that come appear in different costumes, depending on

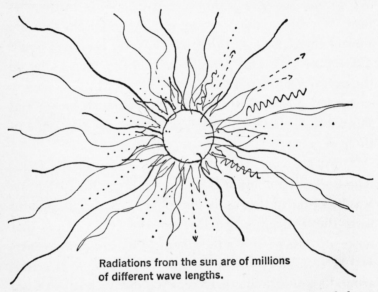

Radiations from the sun are of millions of different wave lengths.

their wave lengths and frequencies. We *see* some of these waves as light, we *feel* some of them as heat, we are kept healthy by others which are called ultraviolet.

We see everything in the world because it either makes or reflects waves of light. Trees *look* green because they reflect light of a certain wave length. Snow *looks* white because it reflects all wave lengths of visible light, and white is a mixture of all wave lengths of what we call color. All the colors that you see are reflections of these light waves, from violet, which has the shortest wave length, to red, which has the longest. When something looks black it is *absorbing,* or taking in, all wave lengths of light.

Wave lengths of light longer than those we see as red color are invisible to us. These waves are called *infra-red.* We cannot see them, but we can feel some of them as heat. We can neither see nor feel wave lengths that are shorter than violet, but they are the most powerful of all. They start with wave lengths just shorter than violet, as the rays we call *ultraviolet.*

We have learned to make radiations much longer and shorter than those which reach us from the sun. One of these is X-ray.

X-rays are very, very short, and the shorter the wave-length of any radiation is, the more powerful is the ray. It is lucky for us that radiations of very short wave lengths from the sun cannot get through the layers of gas that make up the earth's atmosphere. The atmosphere acts as a screen. It is something like the cloud of electrons around a hot cathode that keeps too many electrons from getting through to the plate.

These very short waves from the sun are so powerful that they would destroy most life on earth if they could reach it. We could not control them the way we can control X-rays, because they are thousands of times more powerful. The radiations released by atomic explosions are similar to those very short waves from the sun. One of the jobs of earth satellites is to send back information about the radiations they find in space.

Longer than the waves which we feel as heat are the

electromagnetic waves we make ourselves and call *radio waves* (more about these in Chapter 14). They make possible, among other things, radio and television broadcasting and radar.

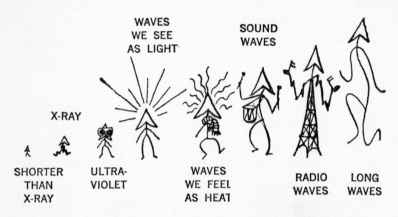

Waves of different lengths appear as different things.

Although sound waves are not electromagnetic, they too have different lengths, and these make all the tones and noises that we hear. When the wave length of a sound is too short we cannot hear it, but it is there all the same. If you've ever had a special dog whistle you know that when you blow it you may not hear a thing, but your dog can hear it distinctly. His ears are tuned to catch sound waves much shorter than you can hear. Very short sound waves have been harnessed to do all sorts of other jobs too.

Some sound waves are too long for your ears to hear. When a violin string is stretched tightly, the note it makes is very high. The looser the string is, the lower the note

Waves

sounds, until finally you don't hear anything at all. But you can *see* the sound as motion. The violin string is vibrating with the sound waves so you know they are there. Sound waves are energy too, with the power to work.

All these waves are an important part of electronics. In electronics we have learned to make use of what we know about each kind of wave. We can make many kinds of radiations, and find and control others.

As we go through the book we'll talk more about these different waves, but now let's take another look at the things we've found out about them.

Waves are started by a disturbance at the source, and radiate out from it.

Some waves are a disturbance traveling through a medium. Some waves do not need a medium at all.

Waves can be reflected, bent or absorbed by something in their path.

The shorter the wave length and the higher the frequency, the more powerful the wave is.

All waves are energy in motion.

Chapter Seven
WHAT ELECTRON TUBES DO

Most of the work of electronics is done by the tubes that regulate the flow of electrons. All of this work is done in the incredibly short space of time that it takes electrons to cross the tube and continue out of it on their way. These tubes are nothing more than a way of getting at the electrons, to speed them up or slow them down, to turn them one way or the other, or to start and stop them, sometimes millions of times a second. There is no way to get at the electrons in a wire to do these things. Electrons in a wire are very hard to control exactly.

An electron tube is really a break in the wire across which electric current flows. The break is enclosed in glass or metal so the air cannot get in. An electron tube is an interruption in the regular flow of electric current

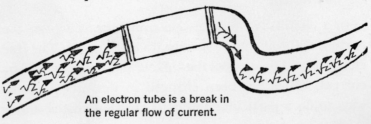

An electron tube is a break in the regular flow of current.

What Electron Tubes Do

through a wire. It can never do anything by itself, but it starts the current flowing in a special way to do a special job. It is rather like the faucet that controls the flow of water in the kitchen sink.

An electron tube is always part of a *circuit*. A circuit is the complete path of an electric current. Electrons are set in motion in a power plant, and as soon as they move together they become electric current. This current travels through wires to its job, does its work, and comes back again to the place where it began. The same electrons are always being used over and over, with fresh pushes through the circuit.

An electron tube is always part of a circuit.

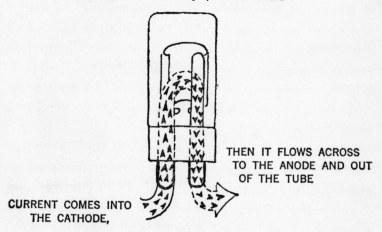

THEN IT FLOWS ACROSS
TO THE ANODE AND OUT
OF THE TUBE

CURRENT COMES INTO
THE CATHODE,

In a circuit of which an electron tube is a part, the current will come into the tube, to the cathode. The free electrons will flow across the tube to the anode. Then the current, which has been changed in the tube in some way, to do a particular job, will flow out of the anode

63

and through another wire to complete the circuit. Sometimes the current does its job in the tube, while it is still free. Sometimes it does its job after it has left the tube and returned to the wire.

No matter when the electrons do their job, the cathode-to-anode circuit has to be completed. Even if the electrons have finished their work in the tube, they have to leave at once so they won't get in the way of other electrons that follow them out of the cathode.

In some tubes, the cathode-to-anode circuit is the only one, but other tubes have to have helper circuits.

A phototube, for instance, does not need a helper circuit, because the light that frees the electrons shines on it from outside the tube and is not connected to it in any way. If the cathode has to be heated, there has to be a second circuit to supply the heat; and if there is a grid in the tube, there must be a third circuit to control the current into the grid.

Since most electron tubes have a hot cathode and an anode and a grid, they must have at least three separate circuits. You can usually tell how many circuits there are in an electron tube by looking at it. You can tell by the little prongs that stick out of the tube. These prongs are called *terminals,* and they are the connection between the tube and the electric circuits. In a phototube, there are only two terminals, one where the current comes into the cathode and another where it leaves the anode.

A tube containing a hot filament and an anode will have three terminals, one for each end of the filament and one for the anode, that completes the circuit.

What Electron Tubes Do

Tubes in which the cathode is separately heated have four terminals. Incoming current flows into two of these

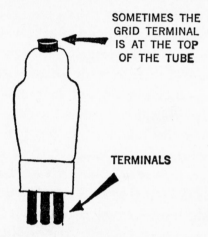

SOMETIMES THE
GRID TERMINAL
IS AT THE TOP
OF THE TUBE

TERMINALS

terminals. One terminal brings electrons to the source and the other supplies the heat to boil them out. The remaining two terminals complete each of these circuits.

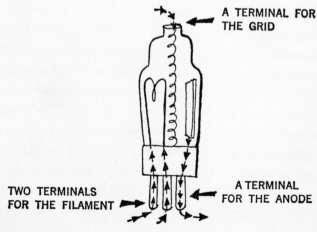

A TERMINAL FOR
THE GRID

TWO TERMINALS
FOR THE FILAMENT

A TERMINAL
FOR THE ANODE

Then, if there is a grid, there will be another prong, which brings in current through the grid. This circuit is completed through the cathode.

When you look at a tube like some of those in your radio, and it has more than five terminals, you have several possibilities to choose from. The tube may have more than one grid, and it must have an extra terminal for each grid. Or the tube may have more than one cathode. If the tube has a regular forest of terminals sticking out of the bottom, it is probably *two* tubes combined in one envelope.

Because current coming into each of the parts of a tube has to do different things, you can see how important it is that these things don't get mixed up.

Electron tubes control the thousands of jobs of electronics by doing just a few things to the current that enters them. Here are those things.

ELECTRON TUBES CONTROL

It is very difficult to control current that is flowing through a wire. Sometimes, for certain work, the current must be turned off and on again thousands of times a minute. It would be very hard to do this with an ordinary switch because the electrons in a conductor like to put themselves to as little trouble as possible. When they are not flowing in a current, they do not want to start, and they have to be given a good push. When they are flowing, they do not want to stop. This is true of everything in the world that moves, and it is called *inertia*. If you

66

What Electron Tubes Do

Electrons in a wire have to be pushed
and pulled to make them start,

and they skid to a stop.

turn off the switch, the electrons still flow a little before
they can skid to a stop. That is when you'll see a spark if
the connection isn't just right.

Starting and stopping the flow of current in a wire so
many thousand times a second would be almost impossible. This is one of the first controlling jobs of an electron tube.

Once the electrons are free in the tube, their flow to
the plate can be stopped or started *millions* of times a
second by the grid. When the grid has enough negative
electricity in it, not one single electron can get through
to the plate. It is just as if a door were slammed in their

Electrons in a tube
can be stopped at
once by the grid.

67

faces, and the current stops immediately. The instant the negative electricity is taken out of the grid, the electrons that have been hanging just as near to it as they could without being bounced off shoot through the grid to the plate, and the current starts again. Since electrons travel almost as fast as light, 186,000 miles a second, you can see how quickly they get across that tiny distance from the grid to the plate. Such amazingly fast changes are hard to imagine, but they happen in electron tubes.

Another job that the tubes do is to control the *amount* of current flowing through a wire. If you just wanted to use half of it, by applying a certain amount of negative voltage to the grid, you could make sure that only half of the electrons got through. If a very constant flow of exactly the same amount of electricity is needed, electron tubes see that no more or less gets through the tube to the wire that carries it on its way.

Electron tubes control the *direction* of the stream of electrons too. In certain tubes that we shall talk about, it is very important that the electrons hit a particular spot or spots on the plate, or move across it in a special way. Electron tubes control the direction of these streams of electrons by making them pass magnets or electromag-

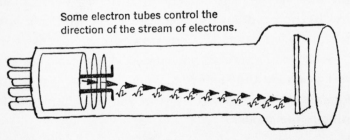

Some electron tubes control the
direction of the stream of electrons.

netic fields. If these fields are positive, the stream of electrons will swing toward them; if they are negative, the stream will swing away from them.

By applying more positive voltage to the plate, the electron tubes can control the *speed* of the electrons through the tube and the *force* with which they hit the plate.

ELECTRON TUBES RECTIFY

Two kinds of electric current flow through our power lines. One kind is known as *direct current,* or d.c., and it is electric current flowing in one direction only. In the other kind, *alternating current,* or a.c., the flow of current changes its direction regularly. First it flows one way, then the other. The current flowing through our power lines is usually alternating, because it is easier to control and cheaper to send over long distances.

But when the current comes to the place where it is to go to work, if direct current is needed something has to make it flow in one direction only, instead of first one way and then the other. When an electron tube is placed in the wire through which alternating current is flowing, the tube *rectifies* the current. It keeps it from changing its direction and flowing backward in the wire, and sends it on its way in a one-way stream of direct current.

Some rectifier tubes are simple. They have no grid, just a cathode and an anode. When the current is flowing forward, it flows straight out of the cathode across the tube to the anode.

What Electron Tubes Do

Free electrons in a tube can flow *one way only*. Because they are always negative, they must flow to the positive

plate. If the plate is made negative, they will stay where they are, but they can never flow backward out of the plate to the cathode. So, when the current in the wire is flowing backward, nothing happens in the tube. The electrons that have already reached the plate stay there. The electrons in the circuit flow backward. Instead of flowing away from the plate and into the cathode, they flow away from the cathode and into the plate. Of course this makes the plate negative and so no current flows across the tube.

Then, when the current in the wire flows forward again, so does the current across the tube. When the current flows out of the tube on the anode side, it is all flowing one way. These was no way for the current going the other way to get into the tube.

ELECTRON TUBES AMPLIFY

Because they are so sensitive to the tiniest amounts of electricity, electron tubes can take a very faint power and build it into much greater power. When these small

What Electron Tubes Do

amounts of power come into the grid they are very weak and they are called signals. This current is called the *signal voltage*. When the strong flow of electrons from the cathode passes across these signals on its way to the plate, the voltage in the grid changes these electrons into its own image, only many times stronger. The weak pattern of voltage that came into the grid has been magnified and strengthened, and that is the way it flows out of the plate.

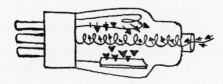

In a high-vacuum tube, weak signals come in on the grid and are magnified

Amplifying valves are found in almost every electronic device.

In some tubes, small amounts of electricity collide with atoms of gas when they leave the cathode. In this collision, electrons are knocked out of the gas atoms, which then form a positive bridge for all the electrons from the

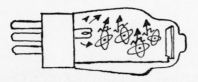

In a gas-filled tube all the electrons cross on a bridge of ions

71

cathode to flow across on their way to the plate. This increases the number of electrons that flow to the plate, because the electrons are not held up on the way.

ELECTRON TUBES GENERATE ALTERNATING CURRENT

Sometimes electron tubes have to change direct current to alternating current of high frequencies, or *oscillations,* as these vibrations are called. The frequency of ordinary alternating current is hardly ever higher than 60 cycles a second. But with oscillator tubes, currents can be made to oscillate thousands or millions of times a second. The oscillator tubes that generate this high-frequency alternating current are really amplifier tubes with their plate circuits connected to their grid circuits in a special way. They also generate the electromagnetic radio waves (or oscillations) that are used in radio broadcasting.

ELECTRON TUBES CONVERT

Electron tubes change one kind of energy into another. An X-ray tube changes electricity into X-rays. Radio tubes change radio waves into electricity and then into sound waves. Some television tubes change electricity into light, others change light into electricity. Phototubes change light into electricity too.

All of the things that are done by electronics are pos-

What Electron Tubes Do

sible only because a tube has done one or more of the things in this chapter.

Many of the things you read about electronics are accompanied by diagrams, and you will find some in the rest of this book. In these diagrams, certain symbols stand for certain parts of the tube or circuit. Here they are.

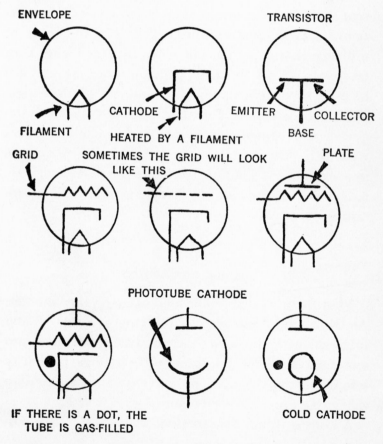

ENVELOPE

TRANSISTOR

CATHODE

EMITTER

COLLECTOR

FILAMENT

HEATED BY A FILAMENT

BASE

GRID

SOMETIMES THE GRID WILL LOOK LIKE THIS

PLATE

PHOTOTUBE CATHODE

IF THERE IS A DOT, THE TUBE IS GAS-FILLED

COLD CATHODE

Chapter Eight
ELECTRONICS
ALL AROUND
YOU

All around you at home are things that work or have been made by electronics. The colors in your paint and wallpaper were matched by a phototube. Your television and radio sets are full of electron tubes. Your telephone and portable radio use transistors. The materials that cover your furniture are evenly woven because of electronics. Your medicine chest is full of things that were electronically packed and inspected, and so are the kitchen cabinets and the refrigerator.

From the time you brush your teeth in the morning (electronics helped fill that tube with toothpaste), until you listen to the bedtime weather report (electronics helps the weatherman with his forecast) your world is filled with electronics.

Those breakfast oranges may have come a great distance to your grocery store. How could the fruit packers know that they were all good before they shipped them? A bad one might spoil the whole crate.

And your breakfast food; how was it packed?

And that picture on the front page of the morning paper—it's of something that happened a few hours ago, halfway around the world. How did it get there? No airplane could fly that fast. Electronics!

Let's suppose you're about to have breakfast. How many times does electronics touch you before you even get up from the table?

Are you eating in the kitchen? You probably switched on the fluorescent lights before you sat down.

Fluorescent lights are electron tubes filled with gas. Instead of plugging in at one end like an ordinary light, they have two terminals at each end that plug into the electric current. Each terminal carries the current into the wires which support the coiled filaments.

A fluorescent light tube has two filaments, one at each end, and the ends of the wires that support those filaments are the anodes. Fluorescent lights are different from other electron tubes because it is not the flow from the filament to the anode that does the main job. That flow just gets the tube started. The main job of a fluorescent lamp is to provide light, and this is how it does it.

Fluorescent lights work on alternating current that keeps flowing back and forth. Since the tube has a filament at each end, there is a constant flow of current into the tube. There is a drop of mercury in the tube that is turned to gas by the electricity coming into the tube. As the electrons flow out of the filaments, they bump into the atoms of mercury vapor, or gas, in the tubes.

When the electrons crash into the atoms of mercury vapor and disturb them, the mercury atoms give off energy in the form of waves of light. These waves are ultraviolet and too short for us to see. The ultraviolet waves radiate out until they hit the inside of the glass envelope.

The inside of the envelope is coated with certain powders called *phosphors,* which are fluorescent. Anything fluorescent will give off radiations when it is absorbing radiations from another source, and that is just what the coating on the inside of these lamps does. It absorbs the ultraviolet radiations we can't see and then gives off

ELECTRONS LEAVING THE FILAMENT BUMP INTO THE
MERCURY GAS ATOMS.

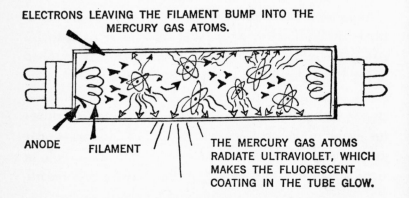

ANODE   FILAMENT   THE MERCURY GAS ATOMS
RADIATE ULTRAVIOLET, WHICH
MAKES THE FLUORESCENT
COATING IN THE TUBE GLOW.

A fluorescent light works like this.

radiations of its own, of a longer wave length, which we see as light.

Different kinds of phosphors radiate different colors of light. That is why some fluorescent lights look blue or pink, white or like sunlight. Because fluorescent lights use phosphors to supply that light they need less current than ordinary electric lights and so they are cheaper to burn.

When you sit down to the table, there is the morning

paper with that picture on the front page. This is part of one of the most exciting miracles of electronics. It is a sort of television, of seeing across space. It traveled through the air across seas and continents. The way it was sent is called *facsimile broadcasting*.

A facsimile is an exact copy, and this exact copy of a picture is recorded in almost the same way that a phonograph record makes a copy of sound. The needle that copied the picture is a needle of light.

Suppose a photographer took a picture of an earthquake in India, and he wanted to send it back to his newspaper office in New York. The picture is wrapped around a cylinder, and the cylinder is revolved on a long screw at an even rate of speed. As the cylinder turns, a needle of light plays across the picture. The light shines on every single spot of the picture as it turns slowly around and up. If you could see the path the needle of light made, it would look like the marks a real recording needle makes on a phonograph record, except that there are no grooves. The whole surface of the picture would be covered with fine lines.

As the light covers the picture, we say it *scans* it. The same word is used in television too.

No other light is allowed to touch the picture. As the light touches each spot, it is reflected back to a phototube. All the different shades of gray and black and white that make up the picture reflect different amounts of light. When these reflections strike the cathode of the phototube they release electrons. The brighter the light shining on the cathode is, the more electrons are released.

THIS NEEDLE OF LIGHT
SCANS THE PICTURE

AND

IS REFLECTED TO
THE PHOTOTUBE.

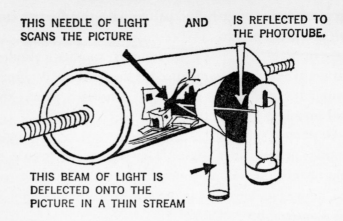

THIS BEAM OF LIGHT IS
DEFLECTED ONTO THE
PICTURE IN A THIN STREAM

As the light scans the picture and is reflected to the cathode, electrons are released that correspond exactly to the shades of light and dark in the picture. These electrons flow across to the anode and the picture leaves the tube as electricity. Since this electricity flows in a definite pattern, it is called a signal.

Another tube amplifies these faint signals and broadcasts them as radio waves. Around the world in New York, a receiver is waiting to pick them up.

When the faint radio signal is picked up and amplified, it goes to the recorder tube. This tube takes the signal with all the variations that were made in the original phototube and changes it back to light.

The recorder tube is coated so that no light can get out of it, except through a special place at the end. This beam of light is *fluctuating*, or vibrating, exactly like the electric current that is coming into the tube. It passes through lenses that narrow it down to another needle of light like the first one. But now, instead of being a steady beam, it is fluctuating with the electric current that is the picture.

In front of this beam of light is another cylinder, turning at exactly the same speed as the first one. Wrapped around the cylinder is a piece of sensitized paper, the kind snapshots are printed on.

All photographic prints are made by variations of light shining on sensitized paper. The fluctuating needle of light records the picture from around the world, and you find it in your morning paper just a few hours after it was photographed.

Another electron tube is always used with the facsimile recorder, one of the tubes that control. This tube keeps the voltage to the recorder tube even. If the voltage changed it would change the electric current that is the picture and the picture would be blurry or distorted.

If you live in a big city, the presses on which your newspaper was printed are electronically controlled. Nobody has to touch the huge rolls of newsprint from the time they go in one end of the press until the newspapers come out the other, printed, folded into pages, and even tied in bundles ready to be delivered to the newsdealer.

If your mail has arrived, some of the letters were probably sorted and the stamps canceled electronically. Electronic mail clerks can even read different kinds of

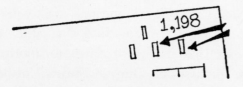

HOLES LIKE THIS
USUALLY MEAN
ELECTRONIC
BOOKKEEPING

handwriting. If there are bills in the mail, some of them were totaled and written electronically by an electronic bookkeeper that even went back and checked itself for errors.

At your place on the table is your orange juice. The oranges were probably inspected by X-ray before they were shipped, to make sure there were no imperfections in them to spoil all the fruit. After your breakfast cereal was packed, its box was inspected by X-ray too, to make sure it was full and free from dirt.

If your bread or milk was *irradiated* it was passed under special ultraviolet lamps. The bread or milk absorbed the ultraviolet rays and will pass it on to you in the form of vitamin D.

Electronics has given you light, news, mail, pure food and sunshine, and your day has just begun.

Chapter Nine
ELECTRONICS
IN INDUSTRY
(Helper with a
Thousand Hands)

THERE ARE hundreds of different electron tubes working in industry, and they do every kind of job. They work in steel mills and in textile mills; they sew and weld and paint and dry. They watch things human eyes could never see, and they count and figure faster than the most brilliant arithmetic student in the world.

The tube that puts in the longest hours in factories is called the *thyratron*. The thyratron is a gas-filled tube with a hot cathode, and it does all sorts of different jobs. One of the most important of these is rectifying alternating current into direct current. Alternating current is the

This diagram of a thyraton shows you all the important things at a glance

most economical to produce, but there are many machines that will not run well on alternating current. The speed of alternating current cannot be controlled as well as that of direct current.

We've talked about a simple rectifier tube that had just a cathode and an anode, but a thyratron has a grid and gas in it besides. Because it has the grid, it can control the flow of current to the anode. A rectifier tube without a grid has no way to stop or start the current flowing across it. And because it has gas in it, the thyratron carries a much heavier flow of current than a high-vacuum tube. Here's why.

In a vacuum tube, the cloud of negative electrons around the cathode keeps other electrons from getting through to the plate

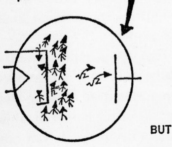

BUT

In a gas-filled tube, the gas ions form a bridge for the electrons to cross in a steady stream

You remember we said that electrons in a high-vacuum tube controlled their own traffic by forming a screen around the cathode. This screen slows down the electron flow across the tube. When gas is used in a tube, this negative screen doesn't get a chance to form around the cathode. The space is filled, instead, with positive gas ions, which pick up the electrons as they leave the cathode.

The gas ions in the tube lead a hard life. Every time they manage to balance themselves with new electrons, more electrons are knocked loose by the rush of current through the tube. Electrons are pushed and pulled from one ion to the next, and so they never get a chance to hold up traffic. There is a constant strong flow of current across the tube, except when the grid purposely interrupts it. That is why most tubes supplying power to heavy industry have gas in them.

The thyratron rectifies a heavy stream of current. Other electron tubes usually control the amount of current in a thyratron. Most electron tubes in industry work in teams with other tubes. Sometimes four or five different kinds work together on a job.

Electronic heating plays a big part in industry today. Food is dehydrated electronically, and paints and enamels are dried the same way. The big advantage of using electronic heat to do these things is speed. Paints or glues that used to take twenty hours to dry properly can now be dried in twenty minutes.

All this is done by the rays we call *infra-red,* which have a wave length just longer than that of visible light. Infra-red rays are usually divided into two groups. The ones that are a bit longer than visible light are called *near* infra-red. A little longer than these are the *far* infra-red rays, which are waves of ordinary heat that can be made in any hot oven.

The reason that near infra-red works so much faster than ordinary heat is that its wave length is shorter and so its radiations are more penetrating. If you were drying the paint on a truck with near infra-red rays, they would penetrate the outside coat of paint to the inside and start drying it all at once. If you were drying the paint with ordinary heat, it would stop at the outside coat and start drying the paint from the outside in. The drier and harder the outside layer of the coat of paint got, the harder it would be for the heat to get through it to dry the paint underneath.

Because near infra-red is shorter than ordinary heat, it is more penetrating.

Infra-red drying ovens are lined with banks of powerful electric lamps. Each lamp has its own reflector, specially made to reflect infra-red rays onto the object to be dried. These reflectors are usually steel, plated with gold.

If you have an electric heater in your house with a reflector behind it, it is reflecting far infra-red, or ordinary, heat waves. One difference between the two kinds of infra-red rays is that far infra-red heats the air as it travels through it, and part of the heat is lost. Near infra-red rays do not heat the air through which they pass, and none of their energy is lost.

Electronics in Industry

Another kind of electronic heating is done by a tube with several grids, called the *pliotron*. The pliotron produces the high-frequency oscillations that we call radio

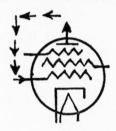

If some of the plate current is fed back to the grid, the tube makes oscillations.

Some pliotrons have several grids.

waves. These waves are used to heat metal and plastic. They pass *through* these things to heat them.

High-frequency heating is also used to glue the layers of plywood together strongly and quickly, and to dry lumber that might take months to dry out by itself.

Multi-grid tubes are also used to generate the large amounts of high-frequency alternating current that most factories use. We usually think of this high-frequency or oscillating current in connection with sending out radio programs. Actually, more high-frequency current is used in industry than in sending out all the radio programs in the world.

X-ray is another of the helpers in industry. Giant industrial X-ray machines may carry a million volts of power and can penetrate inches of solid steel. Then they record what they see on film. This is how we can look at the inside of heavy castings to make sure they have no cracks or holes. We can look through solid steel to see if there are any weak spots.

X-rays do little things in factories too. They look into candy bars, golf balls, cans of food and packages of all kinds. If there is anything wrong, they are marked and rejected by other electron tubes.

The railroads use many electronic devices in running their lines. A nuclear device which shoots out low-voltage gamma rays (you'll read about these later) checks cross ties, beams, electric poles and other wooden structures.

In big railroad freight yards, television screens and computers classify and separate the cars. Electronic devices measure the speed and weight of each car. A computer decides at what speed to "hump" it. Other devices regulate the speed to the exact rate needed to get it over the hump and couple it to the rest of the train.

In some factories electronics does many different separate jobs. But in others, electronics has taken over most

of the job of running things. The word for this is *automation*.

Automation is the use of electronic and mechanical controls to run machinery. It can control a single operation or all the operations in a process. Some machines do the mechanical work of production, others inspect and correct, still others control all the machines involved.

Automation will make many changes in the way we live. It will mean shorter working hours, because things can be manufactured faster with fewer workers. It might mean fewer jobs for unskilled workers, but it will create many new kinds of jobs for workers who learn skills.

In automation the work of many machines is combined so that the processes go smoothly from one step to the next without any human being having to throw switches or make decisions. Control units using X-ray or television picture tubes, photocells or radioactive isotopes (which you'll read about in Chapter 17) are constantly at work, "looking," measuring, making corrections.

Computers, which are often called electronic brains, guide the machines. Computers can receive information and use it at once, or store it for use later. They can even make decisions and carry them out.

In the next chapter we'll talk about these "brains" and how they work.

Chapter Ten
COMPUTERS
(Thinkers for
Industry,
Science
and Defense)

MANKIND's most valuable resource is the human brain. With it man, who is not fast or strong or well-protected by nature, has made himself the ruler of his world. With his brain he can reason, he can calculate and figure things out, he can decide and remember. And using his brain he has invented a mechanical one that can do all these things for him, thousands of times faster than he can.

The only kind of thinking a computer cannot do is original thinking. It has to follow very carefully prepared, orderly directions.

In a way, an electronic brain can be compared to a human brain. There are about ten billion nerves in your brain which relay impulses from one to another at about the speed of sound. The biggest computers have millions of parts—electron tubes, transistors, wires and switches which relay impulses to one another at the speed of light.

A computer can add thousands of figures a second. In one second, some of them can read 70,000 characters.

Computers

Different parts of your brain do different jobs and so do the parts of a computer.

Just as a problem has to come into your brain before you can start thinking about it, the problem to be solved has to be put into the computer. It is put into the part called the *input*.

First, though, the problem has to be "coded," or put into a language the machine understands. Each part of the problem must be in its proper order. Sometimes the

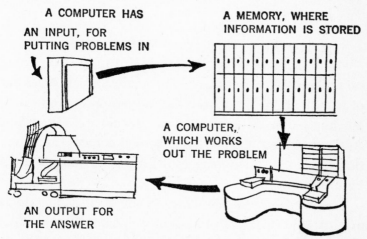

A COMPUTER HAS
AN INPUT, FOR
PUTTING PROBLEMS IN

A MEMORY, WHERE
INFORMATION IS STORED

A COMPUTER,
WHICH WORKS
OUT THE PROBLEM

AN OUTPUT FOR
THE ANSWER

problem is put on punched cards. More often it is recorded on magnetic tape that the machine can "read." Some computers even understand spoken words, and these have microphones in their input.

Preparing a problem and instructions for the computer is called *programming*.

Just as a part of your brain is concerned only with remembering what you have learned, a part of an electronic brain is its "memory."

Computers

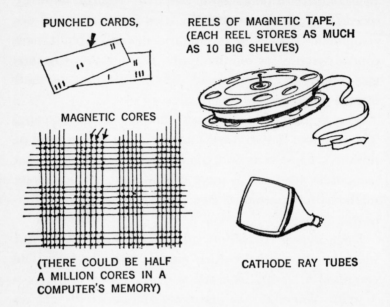

PUNCHED CARDS,

REELS OF MAGNETIC TAPE,
(EACH REEL STORES AS MUCH
AS 10 BIG SHELVES)

MAGNETIC CORES

(THERE COULD BE HALF
A MILLION CORES IN A
COMPUTER'S MEMORY)

CATHODE RAY TUBES

Some computers have facts recorded on magnetic cylinders, some have banks of thousands of tiny magnetic cores, some have reels of magnetic tapes, some have cathode-ray tubes. A computer can reach into its memory to find and use the exact fact it needs in less than a thousandth of a second.

From the memory section, facts are flashed to the computing section, which figures out the answer. Facts from memory are compared, then used or discarded. The computer decides which facts fit the problem and which to discard.

There are two basic kinds of computers, and they do their figuring in different ways.

Computers

The *analogue computer* is a measurer. It may measure and compare differences in current, voltage, heat or speed. Analogue computers are used in research and development. They help develop missiles and aircraft, new control systems for industrial use. Because they can imitate conditions of heat, speed and the like, they are used in many kinds of training devices.

The *digital computer* uses numbers in its figuring. The problem is always fed into the input in the form of numbers, and the answer comes out in numbers. Digital computers are used to solve complicated and elaborate mathematical problems, like those in physics or astronomy.

Some digital computers use the decimal system, but most use the binary (which means "two") system. The computer does all its work with only two numbers— 1 and 0. You could say that these numbers represent yes and no, and the computer is saying yes and no at each step.

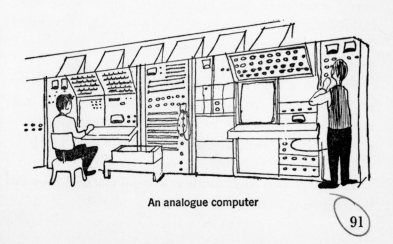

An analogue computer

Computers

All along the way the control system of the computer, which is made of electron tubes and transistors, is at work "reading" instructions and making sure they are carried out correctly.

The final results come out of the *output*. Sometimes the answers are recorded on magnetic tape or punched cards. Some computers print them directly on paper. One kind of computer has an electronic printer that can write almost 5,000 lines of print a minute. It uses the fast scanning of a cathode-ray tube to do the job.

THE OUTPUT IS PRINTED, READY TO BE READ

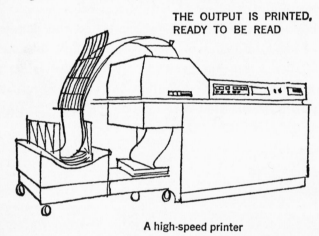

A high-speed printer

Computers do many kinds of work at great speeds. They solve mathematical problems in days, or even hours, that would take mathematicians years to complete.

They control complicated industrial processes.

They translate from one language to another at lightning speeds. They decode ciphers. A computer can break any written code, because it can work its way through all the possible combinations of characters so fast.

Computers

They hear and transcribe messages.

By using and comparing the facts and deciding on the mathematical probabilities, they can make predictions—on elections, sporting events, or even the weather, far in advance. (Here, like any other predicters, sometimes they are wrong!)

In medicine they are used to diagnose disease, working their way swiftly through hundreds of possibilities.

In defense they are used to keep track of millions of supply parts all over the world, to train personnel, and to control guns, planes, rockets and missiles.

They figure satellite orbits, handle all the details of rocket firing and control the satellite's flight into space.

Computers are even used to find their own faults and to design other, better computers. Only your imagination can put limits on what they may do for us in the future.

Chapter Eleven
ELECTRONIC
POLICEMEN

T HE POLICEMEN of the electron family are the phototubes. They are lookouts, watchmen, and detectives. They maintain law and order in the circuits of which they are a part. They count and check and measure and record. Phototubes are the brains of the electron family, but they cannot work without help. They are always part of a team of electron tubes, because the phototube by itself produces such a tiny amount of current that it must be amplified before it can go to work.

A phototube, you remember, is an electron tube with a cold cathode and an anode, but no grid. Sometimes it is a vacuum tube, and sometimes it has gas in it. Electrons are freed from the cathode of a phototube not by heat or strong voltage but by light. This light comes from outside the tube, and it is the energy that crashes into the cathode and knocks the electrons out of it. The bits of energy that make up all light waves are called *photons*.

LIGHT
FREES
ELECTRONS

EACH ELECTRON
SPLASHES OUT
OTHERS WHEN
IT HITS

Electronic Policemen

The source in a phototube is usually a curved sheet of metal, coated with a material that will give off electrons easily when it is bombarded with photons of light. The kind of coating usually depends on the wave lengths of light that are going to be turned on it. Different light-sensitive materials give off more electrons when they are hit with certain wave lengths of light.

Some phototubes even work on invisible light, light with wave lengths of ultraviolet or infra-red. Zinc is sensitive to ultraviolet, calcium to ordinary light, potassium to blue light.

After the electrons leave the cathode, they are pulled toward the positive anode, which is a metal rod standing equally distant from all parts of the curved source. The electrons then flow out into the circuit as electric current. Light has been changed into electricity.

There is one phototube that amplifies its own current. This tube has several anodes. The electrons leave the cathode and bounce to the first anode. But the positive voltage there isn't very high; and, as the electrons hit it, they splash out more electrons, and then they all flow together to the second anode, which has a slightly higher voltage. If each electron splashes out half a dozen more when it hits, you can see that the current has increased. By the time the always-growing number of electrons have bounced past several anodes, they hit the final one in a current strong enough to do some jobs without the help of an amplifier tube. These tubes are used where a great deal of current is not necessary and it is important to save space.

Electronic Policemen

The first cousin of the phototube is the photocell. This can be a bulb or a small metal disk that is sensitive to light and can change it into electricity.

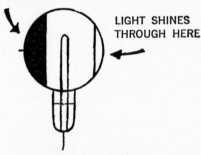

PHOTOSENSITIVE COATING

LIGHT SHINES THROUGH HERE

A photocell looks like this

Some phototubes have gas in them, and some are high-vacuum tubes. Gas-filled phototubes will work on much fainter beams of light, because they make sure that the very few electrons leaving the cathode are convoyed safely to the anode without being held up. Besides, the gas atoms in the tube add a few electrons of their own.

This is why only high-vacuum tubes can be used where the beam of light must be changed into its *exact* portrait in electricity. If there were gas in the tube and the current were changed in the smallest way, the picture would be wrong.

The strange part about most phototubes is that they see, not when the beam of light is shining, but when it is *broken*. As soon as the beam of light is broken, it is a signal to the assistant tube working with the phototube to get to work.

96

Electronic Policemen

For instance, here is how a burglar alarm works. A beam of light is stretched across doors, windows, or a passageway or flight of steps that a burglar must pass. The light is invisible, of course. If the burglar could see it, he would just step over or stoop under it.

The beam shines across the passageway onto the cathode of a phototube. It keeps electrons flowing across the

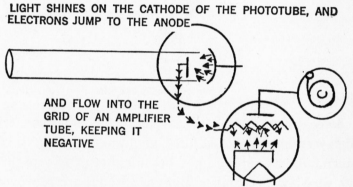

LIGHT SHINES ON THE CATHODE OF THE PHOTOTUBE, AND ELECTRONS JUMP TO THE ANODE

AND FLOW INTO THE GRID OF AN AMPLIFIER TUBE, KEEPING IT NEGATIVE

AS LONG AS THE GRID STAYS NEGATIVE NO ELECTRONS CAN GET TO THE PLATE TO SOUND THE ALARM.

A burglar alarm works like this.

phototube, out of the anode, and into the grid circuit of the amplifier tube that is working as its assistant. As long as this negative current is flowing into the grid of the amplifier tube, the grid keeps electrons in that tube from crossing to the plate.

But when the burglar moves along the passageway, he crosses the invisible beam of light and breaks it. As soon as the light is broken, the current across the photo-tube stops. As soon as that current stops, no more negative current flows into the grid of the assistant tube. Now the electrons in that tube can pass the grid and complete the circuit. And the current flowing out of the tube sets off the burglar alarm.

Magic fountains and doors that seem to open and shut by themselves work exactly the same way. As soon as the beam of light is broken—on the door by someone coming up to it, on the fountain by your head as you bend down for a drink—current flows across the amplifier tube that opens the door or starts the water in the fountain.

Phototubes are the policemen that turn on street and highway lights in most big cities. Ordinary daylight supplies the light that keeps the current flowing through the phototube. When evening comes and it gets too dark for that light to work, the current through the tube stops and allows the flow of current through the amplifier tube to turn on the lights. That is why, during a bad storm, the lights go on even though it isn't night. There is not enough daylight to keep them turned off.

Phototubes are firewardens too. Automatic power relay stations, for instance, have no people working in them, so a fire could start unnoticed. But the rising smoke would break the beam of light and sound the alarm.

In some factories, phototubes are the safety policemen on machines. They stand guard in front of sharp blades or saws or heavy punchers. If a finger or a hand or even a bit of clothing gets near enough to break the light beam, the current stops the machine in a split second.

Phototubes are good counters and measurers. No matter how fast things are moving past, the phototube can count them, as long as there is a little space between. The beam of light will go off and on, and every time it is broken the signal will go back that says, "Something is passing." The assistant tube amplifies this signal and uses it to pull a lever or make a mark that will record the things that are passing.

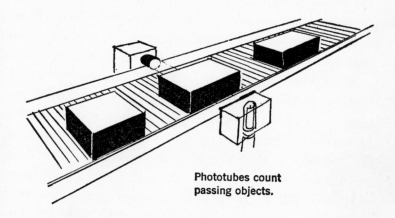

Phototubes count passing objects.

Because they are so sensitive to light and its different wave lengths, phototubes are good measurers and sorters of color. Your eyes can see the differences between ten thousand shades and tints of color. That seems like a lot. But an electronic device with a phototube in it can pick out *two million* different shades, because it reacts to the faintest changes in the wave lengths of these colors. You can see how important this would be to the people who manufacture paints or paper, or dye fabrics or tint china, where all the colors must match exactly. The electron lookout keeps them from making a mistake.

99

Electronic Policemen

Electric eyes can see pinholes in sheets of metal, or the smallest impurities in the air or water. Every gas or chemical in the world reflects its own special wave length of light, and the phototube picks up these wave lengths and signals them to its helper tube.

A phototube and a thyratron are a team.

The thyratron is the tube that usually works with the phototube. Between them, they are a detective and police force that is hard to beat.

Chapter Twelve
ELECTRONICS
GUARDS YOUR
HEALTH

ELECTRONICS stands guard over your health. It watches to see that the food you get is pure. It adds health-giving radiations to some foods and checks others for harmful radioactivity. It sterilizes both the things you eat and the containers in which they are packed. It checks the water and milk you drink and the air around you in public places and out of doors.

If you should get sick, electronics helps your doctor and hospital to get you well as fast as possible.

Probably the best known of these electronic helpers in medicine are the X-rays.

When we were talking about radiations we said that the shorter their wave length is, the more powerful the wave is. Visible light waves are shorter than heat, ultraviolet waves are shorter than visible light, and X-rays are shorter and more powerful than ultraviolet. But even X-rays are not as powerful as the rays given off by radium.

These radium rays are called *gamma rays*. They are so powerful that the tiniest crumbs of radium are kept in thick lead boxes so they cannot injure people who come near them. (Lead absorbs radioactivity.) A bit of radium will go on giving off these rays for thousands of years and nothing can stop it.

New radioactive substances, artificially made, are easier to control than radium. These are proving tremendously important in the study and cure of many diseases.

X-rays are made by man too, so they can be turned off and on, directed and controlled. They have special powers that make them useful to us.

X-rays can pass through many solids that visible light cannot penetrate.

They cause fluorescent materials to give off light.

Although their light is not visible, they affect photographic plates and make them record the pictures we know as X-ray films.

Some X-rays can destroy living tissue, so they can be used to kill cancer cells. Exposure to X-rays can also *transmute* or change cells and produce new kinds of living things. New flowers and sturdier kinds of grain have been made by turning X-rays on their seeds.

An *X-ray tube* produces X-rays. A stream of electrons is made to cross the tube in a thin beam that will hit a certain spot on the anode with great force. The cathode in an X-ray tube is a fine wire filament with a metal cup over it. The metal cup acts as a grid and focuses the electrons into a beam.

If you pasted a black paper over the end of your flash-

light and cut just a tiny hole in the center of the paper, the light would come out in a thin, concentrated beam. That is the way electrons come out of the focusing cathode of an X-ray tube.

Since the voltage in the anode of an X-ray tube is very high, the beam of electrons is yanked toward it with great force. The anode of an X-ray tube is usually made of copper. The electron beam is not supposed to hit the whole anode but a special part of it called the *target*. The target is made of tungsten, a metal that has a very high melting point. (Filaments in electric light bulbs are made of tungsten, too.)

ELECTRON GUN

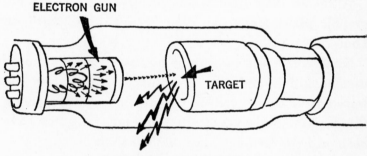

TARGET

An X-ray tube looks like this.

To get good X-rays, the beam must hit a very fine point on the target. Of course, if the beam kept hitting that same spot with such power, it would start to melt, so in some tubes the anode is rotated and the beam keeps hitting different parts of the target. In other tubes, oil or water is kept circulating behind the target to cool it.

The electrons flying in a beam across the tube are stopped suddenly by the target, and they hit it with such

103

speed and force that the electrons in the target are shaken out of place. The waves of energy released by these electrons as they try to regain their positions are called X-rays.

If the doctor just wanted to *see* what was happening inside of any part of you, he would put you between the X-ray machine and a fluorescent screen. The X-rays would pass through you and make a picture in light on the fluorescent screen, by causing it to give off its own rays where it was struck by the X-rays. Where there was just flesh, more X-rays would have passed through you. Where there was bone, fewer would. The picture on the screen would be an exact shadow copy of how you look inside. This is called *fluoroscopy*.

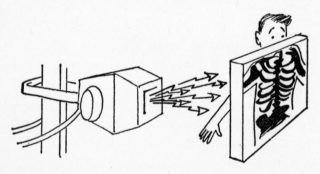

Locating something a baby had swallowed, for instance, would be easy, because its shadow would be right there for the doctor to see.

If he wanted to take a picture instead of just looking at the shadow on the fluorescent screen, he would use a photographic plate instead. The X-rays passing through the baby would make a shadow picture on the film that the doctor could study. This is called *radiography*.

Electronics Guards Your Health

In another chapter we talked about an oscillator tube, which produces the high-frequency radio waves which are used in industry to pass an electric current through an object and heat it from the inside. In medicine, the pliotron is used the same way. Its use in medicine is called *diathermy*.

Because the length of these radio waves can be regulated, heat can be made in any part of the body without burning the skin. An artificial fever can be made to burn up infections that cannot be reached from the outside.

Other waves are used in electronic medicine too. Ultraviolet lamps can give you, in a few minutes, the good of days of sunshine. Ultraviolet is also an important help in packing drugs, medicines, and bandages.

Ultraviolet sterilizing lamps are filled with the mercury gas that gives off ultraviolet rays when the electrons flowing through the tube bump into the gas atoms. Alternating current flows back and forth the way it does in a fluorescent lamp. The envelope, though, instead of being coated inside with fluorescent powders, is made of quartz or a special glass that will allow ultraviolet rays to pass through it. Ultraviolet rays cannot travel through ordinary glass. That is why you can never get a sunburn through a closed window, even if the sun is shining directly on you. When bandages and other medical supplies are sterilized and then packed, ultraviolet lamps keep new bacteria from getting in during packaging. When you get them, they are completely sterile.

Infra-red radiations are used medically for applying

soothing heat to sprains and bruises where the more penetrating radio waves are not needed.

The very penetrating rays of radium are used for controlling cancer, and medical science has a great new can-
cer-fighting tool in some of the radio isotopes produced
by the release of atomic energy.

Amplifier tubes are important medical assistants. The
electrocardiograph records the minute electrical current

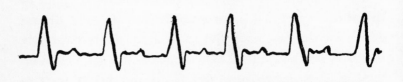

YOUR HEARTBEAT MAKES A DRAWING
ON AN ELECTROCARDIOGRAPH

that is generated when your heart beats, and traces a
picture of this current onto a paper for the doctor to look
at. The electronic stethoscope magnifies the sound of your
heart until it is loud enough for a number of doctors
to hear at once. A doctor can tell a lot of things from the
sound of your heartbeat.

Another device, the electroencephalogram, is so sensitive that it can measure and record the very faint electric currents that flow in your brain. Some diseases cause
changes in the pattern of this current.

Dentists use more and more electronic equipment too.
Almost everyone has had his teeth X-rayed in a dentist's
office, but have you seen these things?

Electronics Guards Your Health

An electronic sterilizer that sterilizes instruments at much greater heats than steam?

A high-speed drill that drills out cavities so quickly that you don't feel any pain? This drill works so fast that it has a fine water spray attached, to keep the drill and your teeth from getting too hot.

A high-speed oscillator for cleaning your teeth? It vibrates so fast—over a thousand times a second—that it actually shakes the tartar off your teeth in a fine powder.

The *electron microscope,* which we shall talk about in the next chapter, has made it possible to see some disease germs for the first time and to enlarge others so greatly that they can be studied. When doctors can get a close-up view of these germs, they can figure out better ways to fight them.

Chapter Thirteen
ELECTRONICS
LENDS A HAND
TO SCIENCE

FOR A LONG TIME the microscope has been one of science's most important assistants. With a modern, high-power microscope we can magnify things more than two thousand times.

A microscope works like this. A strong beam is made by passing a powerful light through a lens. This beam of light is focused on the object to be studied under the microscope. This object is called the *specimen*.

Sometimes the specimen is very thin and translucent, which means that light can pass through it. The beam of light, passing through the specimen, makes a light-and-shade picture of it that falls on another lens. A small part of this image is then enlarged again, and that is the image you finally see.

This type of microscope has one drawback that has prevented scientists from studying many things they would like to see. To understand this difficulty we have to go back to some of the things we said about light waves.

Everything you see is a reflection of waves of light. Compared to some other kinds of waves, light waves aren't very short. Some of the things that scientists want to look at are actually as small as or smaller than waves of light.

It is hard to imagine that though thousands of light waves together may not be an inch long, there are many disease germs so much smaller than waves of light that scientists have never seen them.

We would also like to study the patterns that molecules make in different kinds of matter. This may give us clues as to how these kinds of matter are made up. Since some

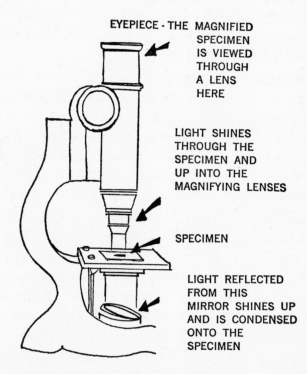

EYEPIECE - THE MAGNIFIED SPECIMEN IS VIEWED THROUGH A LENS HERE

LIGHT SHINES THROUGH THE SPECIMEN AND UP INTO THE MAGNIFYING LENSES

SPECIMEN

LIGHT REFLECTED FROM THIS MIRROR SHINES UP AND IS CONDENSED ONTO THE SPECIMEN

A microscope works like this. (Read from the bottom up.)

molecules are only a few atoms together, they are much too small to be actually seen. Waves of light are gigantic by comparison.

There are some things that we can see with a light microscope but not clearly enough to study or photograph.

The electron microscope has solved many of these problems.

Substituting electrons for light, scientists can now magnify things to a hundred-thousand times their actual size. A freckle could look as large as a landing field and the vein of a leaf larger than the biggest tree in the world. Because they have traded beams of electrons for beams of light, scientists can see things they only imagined before.

An electron microscope works like this.

Up at the top is an electron gun—a hot cathode covered by an anode with a small hole in the center. The electrons shoot out of this hole in a beam that takes the place of the light beam in an ordinary microscope. There are no glass lenses in an electron microscope. Instead, magnetic fields are used to focus the beam of electrons. These magnetic lenses do the same thing to the electron beam that the glass lenses do to the beam of light.

When the electron beam shoots out of the gun, it passes through the magnetic lens, which is a coil of wire shaped like a doughnut. The magnetic lens focuses it onto the specimen. As the electrons strike the specimen, more or fewer pass through it, depending on its density

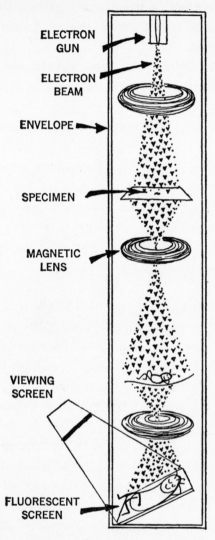

ELECTRON GUN

ELECTRON BEAM

ENVELOPE

SPECIMEN

MAGNETIC LENS

VIEWING SCREEN

FLUORESCENT SCREEN

An electron microscope works like this. A beam of electrons is used instead of light.

at the place they hit. They come out the other side in an electron pattern of the specimen.

This pattern is refocused and enlarged, and then a small part of that enlargement is enlarged *again* by another magnetic lens. This final electron enlargement is projected onto a fluorescent screen which gives off light when the electrons hit it—more light where there are lots of electrons and less where the specimen was too dense to let many through.

If the scientists wanted to photograph the specimen, they would use a photographic plate instead of a fluorescent screen. A special pump keeps all the air pumped out of the electron microscope, so there won't be any air atoms to deflect the beam.

You can picture the stages by which the electron microscope enlarges the specimen if you imagine that you are looking at a house through a giant telescope. The house would fill the whole lens. Then, if you refocused it, the door would fill the lens, as large as the house looked before. When you focused it again, all you could see would be the keyhole, but as big as the door and as big as the house looked to begin with.

Just as the electron microscope is a mighty assistant to science and medicine, a new kind of telescope, one that doesn't see but "hears" the stars, is opening new worlds in astronomy.

Many stars are not visible, even through the most powerful optical telescope. Some stars are much too far away. Billions of them are hidden from view by dust, or clouds of gases. Many stars are not luminous at all. They

Electronics Lends a Hand to Science

do not give off any light but they do emit powerful radio waves. Astronomers call these radio stars, and they are common throughout the universe.

A radio telescope is really a large aerial, set in the center of an immense, bowl-shaped reflector. The biggest radio telescope in the world, at Joddrel Bank in England, has a reflector so large that 10,000 people could sit in it. But it can be delicately controlled to move a fraction of an inch in any direction.

A radio telescope can "tune in" on stars millions of

REFLECTOR

The giant radio telescope at Jodrell Bank, England

light years away. (A light year is the distance light, or electromagnetic waves, can travel in a year. You can find out how far this is by multiplying the distance light travels in a second—186,000 miles—by the number of seconds in a year.) Scientists think that with the radio telescope they will be able to "see" to what they calculate now to be the limits of the universe. This is a distance of two million million light years.

Another electronic device that has lent a helping hand to science is the *strobotron*. The strobotron is a cold cathode tube filled with gas. Among other uses, it supplies the brilliant light that is used in making the extremely high-speed, stop-action pictures we call *stroboscopic* photography.

You have probably seen stroboscopic pictures—a single drop of milk falling into a pan, a football at the split second it was kicked, a bullet hitting a sheet of glass. These pictures show clearly and exactly things that happen too fast for human eyes to study.

To get these pictures, which are actually a series of still pictures of a complete motion, it is necessary to have a light that will flash off and on distinctly thousands of times a second. Each time the light flashes on, a picture is taken of the next stage of the motion. If the light stayed on, the picture would be just one big blur of the action.

Electronics Lends a Hand to Science

You can see why the light must be electronic. In an ordinary electric light, the filament would not get cool enough to stop glowing and giving off light in a hundredth of a second. Even in a fluorescent lamp, which is electronic, the fluorescent coating inside the tube gives off light waves after the current has been turned off.

In the strobotron, the electrons flow into a sort of electric reservoir called a *condenser*. When the condenser is full it overflows, and the electrons combine with the gas atoms in the tube in a great flash of light. These flashes can be controlled exactly, and they take the place of the shutter in ordinary photography. When the light is on, it is as if the shutter were open, and the picture is exposed. When the light goes off, the exposure is over.

The fastest shutter on an ordinary camera is 1/1,200 of a second, but a strobotron flash can take a picture in a millionth of a second.

The fastest shutter on a camera takes 1/1,200 of a second to open and shut.

BUT

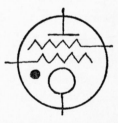

A strobotron tube can control a flash of 1/1,000,000 of a second.

Stroboscopic pictures have been very important in the study of what happens to machinery moving at rapid speeds. Airplane propellers, for example, can be designed better if the designers can study the strain that high speeds put on them. Pictures that show the propeller clearly in every position of its turn help.

Oceanographers use stroboscopic cameras for underwater photography, too.

Meteorologists now use electronics to help forecast the weather. Transmissometers measure visibility. Ceilometers measure cloud height. An infra-red absorption hygrometer measures fog formations. A telesychrometer system measures humidity. A special receptor called "Radiosonde" measures temperature, relative humidity, pressure and wind velocity aloft.

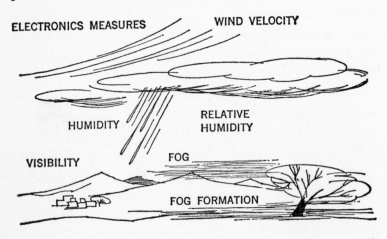

Radar (you'll read more about this in Chapter 16) is a great weather assistant. It can even spot the image of a tornado 200 miles away, so the weather bureau has time to broadcast warnings. Large weather bureaus use computers, too, for long-range forecasting. The computer takes all the known statistics for the weather on a certain day, all the present and short-range conditions, and can generally predict what the weather will be like.

Another of science's assistants is the Geiger counter. Geiger counters are used to detect and measure radioactivity. Some Geiger counters are made with transistors. They all contain a gas-filled electron tube.

When the gas atoms are complete, no electricity flows through the tube. But when the counter is exposed to radioactivity, the radiations ionize the gas atoms by knocking electrons out. This makes current flow through the tube, causing the clicking noises that tell when radioactivity is present.

When we can measure radioactivity, we can learn the ages of rocks and the earth, the presence of uranium or oil, the purity of the air, how plants use minerals, cosmic rays in space, and many, many other things.

Scientists are now doing something men have dreamed about for thousands of years. They are changing the elements themselves. They can change one element to another, and even create new ones—elements a million times more precious than gold. (More about these in Chapter 17.)

Chapter Fourteen
ELECTRONICS
ENTERTAINS
YOU—RADIO
AND THE
MOVIES

T HE FLEMING VALVE, the first modern electron
tube, was a radio tube. In radio, electronics has
done one of its biggest jobs.

Your radio is a bridge between you and the world. It
is always open to bring you news, entertainment, and
music. It is ready at the flip of a switch. Radio has come a
long way since the Fleming valve, and out of that first
radio tube has grown the whole field of electronics.

Radio waves are very complicated things. They start
out in the wire as electrons flowing in a pattern, like
waves. But the up and down of the wave is really just more
electrons, or less, flowing through the wire. This current
in the wire is called a *signal*.

When radio signals leave the wire and are broadcast,
they stop being electric current and start being electromagnetic waves. These waves are very mysterious. We
can make them, find them and control them, but we don't
know what they really are.

Radio waves have wave lengths that start just longer
than infra-red, and get longer until they reach the length

of sound waves. Different lengths of radio waves are used for different things. The radio waves that are used in radar are quite short. Television waves are a little longer.

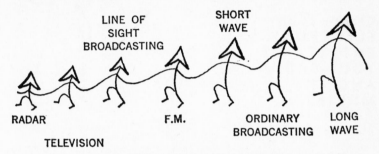

LINE OF SIGHT BROADCASTING   SHORT WAVE

RADAR   F.M.   ORDINARY BROADCASTING   LONG WAVE

TELEVISION

Radio waves come in assorted sizes.

Then come the waves used for short-distance or line-of-sight broadcasting, then those used for FM, then the waves used for long-distance broadcasting. After this come the waves used in regular broadcasting, and then come long waves, which are almost a mile long.

All waves radiate outward from their source. Ordinary long radio waves start out from the broadcasting antenna quite strongly, but as they travel out in all directions, they use up more and more of their energy. Some of them keep traveling, though, until they hit a layer of gas which surrounds the earth and which is so charged with electricity that it acts like a mirror and reflects the waves back to earth. This gas layer is called the *ionosphere*. Its electricity comes from some of the waves of energy sent out by the sun.

Ordinary long radio-broadcasting waves hit the lowest layer of the ionosphere and bounce back to earth where they bounce on for a short distance. But as the waves get shorter, they go farther and still farther through the ionosphere before they are reflected back to earth. Therefore these higher-frequency waves make much longer bounces, covering hundreds of miles at each bounce. That is why the shorter waves are used for long-distance broad-

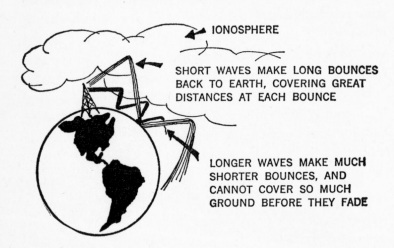

IONOSPHERE

SHORT WAVES MAKE LONG BOUNCES BACK TO EARTH, COVERING GREAT DISTANCES AT EACH BOUNCE

LONGER WAVES MAKE MUCH SHORTER BOUNCES, AND CANNOT COVER SO MUCH GROUND BEFORE THEY FADE

casting. The very high-frequency waves, which we'll talk about later, go right through the ionosphere, and only on very rare occasions ever get back to earth at all.

The air around you is always full of radio waves being broadcast by different stations everywhere. So that the radio waves from one station will not get mixed up with the waves from another, each station is given its own particular frequency, and it is not allowed to broadcast radio waves of any other frequencies.

Sometimes you hear of one country *jamming* the broadcasts of another country. Both are broadcasting at the same wave lengths and frequencies, so that the news broadcast cannot be picked up without getting the jamming broadcast right along with it.

This is how you can pick out one station from all the programs that are being broadcast. When you turn the dial on your radio to a certain station, you are putting your receiving set in *resonance* with the station that is broadcasting those particular radio waves. That means you are tuning it to vibrate to the exact wave length and frequency of the station that is sending out the waves.

Have you ever made a glass on the dinner table ring by hitting it accidentally with a piece of silver, and heard another glass on the table sing out the same note? Those

The glasses are in resonance.

two glasses were in resonance with each other. They were tuned to vibrate to exactly the same wave length of sound. The sound waves left the glass you hit and traveled outward to the other glass. When they hit the other glass, it vibrated and produced the same note.

In the same way, radio waves travel outward from the station in which they are made and are picked up by

121

any receiving sets that are tuned in resonance with them. The first glass you hit was like the antenna of a radio station, and the second glass was the receiving set.

The radio waves that are picked up by your receiver start as sound waves entering a microphone. These waves have a definite pattern of loudness, softness and frequency. The vibration of these sound waves hits a very sensitive disk, or *diaphragm,* in the microphone and makes it vibrate. The disk is connected to an electric current so that the disk's vibrations make an electric pattern like the pattern of the sound waves. The sound waves have been changed into electricity.

Sound waves make the diaphragm vibrate.

This fluctuating pattern of current, which is called the *audio signal,* travels out of the microphone through a wire to the control room, where it is amplified and sent through more wires to the station transmitter. Here it is amplified again but it is still not strong enough to travel long distances by itself.

Meantime, oscillator tubes in the transmitter have been making the high-frequency current that is going to carry the weak audio signal. The two currents are mixed

122

and broadcast together. The strong current becomes the *carrier wave* which carries the other to your radio. When this high-frequency current is mixed with the audio signal, we say it has been *modulated*.

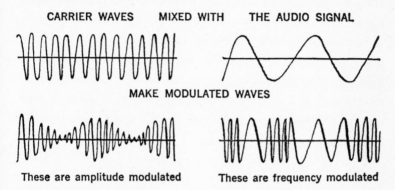

CARRIER WAVES   MIXED WITH   THE AUDIO SIGNAL

MAKE MODULATED WAVES

These are amplitude modulated   These are frequency modulated

From the transmitter, the radio waves are sent to the antennas, which are very tall towers sticking up above the surrounding countryside or buildings. The radio waves then radiate out from the antennas in all directions.

In your house, you have just tuned your radio to that station and put it in resonance with the broadcasting frequency. Your radio receiver picks up the right waves at once, and feeds these signals into an amplifying tube through the grid. When they come into your set, the signals are so faint that they must be amplified a million times or more before you can hear them. An exact but much stronger duplicate of the radio signal that came in on the grid flows out of the plate of the amplifying tube.

Up to this point the high-frequency current that has carried the audio signal is still mixed with it. Now it is

123

the job of special tubes called *detector tubes* to sift the carrier current out and send just the audio signal on its way. This signal is now of *audio frequency* which means that it is vibrating slowly enough to be changed into sound. Perhaps you wonder why the two currents have to be separated. The reason is that a high-frequency wave vibrates much too fast to be translated into sound.

This audio-frequency current is now amplified, and flows into the diaphragm of the loud-speaker, making it vibrate. And these vibrations of the loud-speaker make the sound waves you hear.

All this has happened so fast that you actually hear the sounds coming out of your radio at the same time the people in the broadcasting station hear them. You might even hear the sounds a fraction of a second before, because radio waves travel 186,000 miles a second, and the ordinary sound waves that the studio audience is listening to travel only 1,100 feet a second. The radio waves flash across the country to you faster than the sound waves can get to the other end of the studio.

The radio waves we've talked about so far have been AM, or *amplitude modulated.*

The amplitude of a wave is the up-and-down distance between the highest part, or crest of a wave, and the lowest part, or trough.

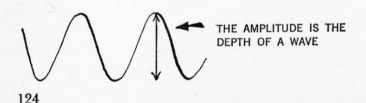

THE AMPLITUDE IS THE
DEPTH OF A WAVE

Electronics Entertains You—Radio and the Movies

There are two disadvantages to amplitude modulation. One is that the wave bands which the Federal Communications Commission assigns to the different radio stations are very close together. This limits the range of sounds you can hear in waves that have been amplitude modulated, because if the waves ranged high or low enough to carry all of these sounds, waves of one station would interfere with waves broadcast by the station on the adjoining band.

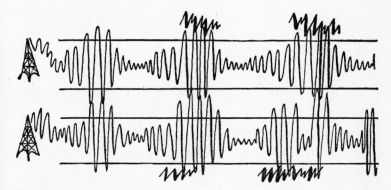

Another disadvantage is that static impulses are amplitude modulated, too, and ride straight into your set as nonpaying passengers. You can't slice them off the edges without slicing away the signal too.

Major E. F. Armstrong developed a new way of broadcasting by modulating the frequency instead of the amplitude of the carrier wave.

Frequency-modulated, or FM, waves carry signals, not by varying the amplitude of the carrier waves, but by changes in the frequency or number of vibrations in a second.

125

FM waves need great amplitude to carry the larger range of tones that they do. Because of this, and because they shift frequency and would get mixed up with other broad-

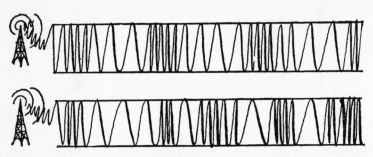

casts, there is no room for them on the regular broadcast band. That is why they have a band of their own. Special tubes in FM radio sets slice away the static-carrying tops and bottoms of the waves. Even in a bad thunderstorm you don't hear any noise.

Electronics is with you when you go to the moving pictures, too. Moving-picture sound is made electronically. This sound is not a record being played. It is a picture right on the film with the movie itself.

The sound track, as it is called, may be one of two kinds. It may be a wavy little line, covering more or less of the area at the edge of the film, or it may be a wider, even line that is more dense in some spots and less in others. Some parts will be quite dark and allow very little light through, and some parts will be quite thin, allowing lots of light to pass. You can see both kinds of sound track in the picture on the next page.

Both these sound tracks are a picture of sound. The sound waves have gone into a microphone and were

126

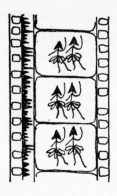

This is called a variable area sound track.

This is called a variable density sound track.

changed there into a fluctuating electric current that matches them exactly. Then this current is used to record a pattern of light and dark areas on the film, which matches the pattern of the sound waves.

In your theater, the pattern on the film is changed back to a pattern of light, then to one of electricity, and finally to sound.

The sound track on the film is run between a beam of light and a phototube. Where a lot of light can get through the film to the phototube, a lot of electrons will be released from the cathode of the tube. Where the film is dense, or where more of the sound track is covered, less light will get through, and fewer electrons will be released to flow across the tube.

The electrical picture of the sound track then flows out of the tube into an amplifier, which magnifies the current until it is strong enough to vibrate the loud-speaker. These vibrations in the loud-speaker change the fluctuating current to sound, and you hear it while you are seeing the picture.

Another way of recording sound is on a magnetic wire or tape. This kind of recording device has the advantage of being very mobile, as all the necessary equipment can be carried in a small case. Besides this, the recording can be played back immediately to determine whether any additions or changes are needed.

The tape is run through an electromagnet, which is fed by current from the recorder's microphone, and so is magnetized to a greater or less degree. The sounds coming into the microphone are accurately recorded in this way. The same tape may be used over and over until a satisfactory recording is made, as it can be wiped clean instantly by a demagnetizing coil.

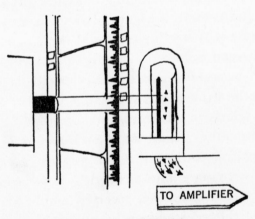

TO AMPLIFIER

This is how the sound track is changed back to electricity.

Chapter Fifteen
ELECTRONICS ENTERTAINS YOU— TELEVISION

O^F ALL the things electronics does, television seems the most magical, because with television we can see across space. We can sit in our homes and theaters and watch things miles away from us as they happen.

Television pictures are sent in a way similar to the broadcasting of still pictures for your newspaper, but with an important difference. When that still picture is broadcast, there is plenty of time to scan and send it, because it is standing still and must only be recorded. Television is the broadcasting of a moving scene, and it must be scanned and broadcast fast enough to keep up with the action as it is happening.

A television camera looks something like a movie camera from the outside, but there is no film in it. Instead of being recorded on film, the picture enters the camera and is changed into electricity. It is broadcast, picked up by your television receiver, amplified, turned back into light again, and you see it at last as a picture on the screen of your receiver. All this happens so fast that you see the picture and hear the sound at the very moment they are being broadcast.

Electronics Entertains You—Television

Many different electron tubes work in television, but the foreman of them all is the tube that is the heart of the television camera. This tube is called an *orthicon,* and it is one of the most complicated tubes in electronics.

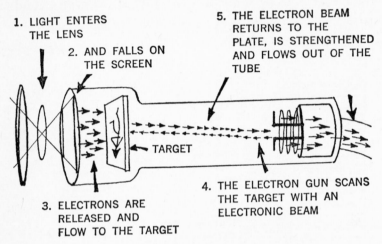

1. LIGHT ENTERS THE LENS

2. AND FALLS ON THE SCREEN

3. ELECTRONS ARE RELEASED AND FLOW TO THE TARGET

4. THE ELECTRON GUN SCANS THE TARGET WITH AN ELECTRONIC BEAM

5. THE ELECTRON BEAM RETURNS TO THE PLATE, IS STRENGTHENED AND FLOWS OUT OF THE TUBE

TARGET

How an orthicon works

The picture is focused by the lens of the camera, and falls on the light-sensitive screen at one end of the orthicon tube. This screen is made of thousands of tiny chemically coated spots, and as light falls on each of them, it releases electrons. The brighter the light that hits each spot, the more electrons it sends out.

The electrons flow back to another screen called the target, releasing still more electrons. As these electrons are released they are collected and sent out of the tube, leaving the target with a strong positive charge, hungry for electrons.

At the other end of the orthicon is an electron gun,

shooting a beam of electrons at the target. The beam moves swiftly back and forth across the target from left to right the way you read a book, but much, much faster. This is called *scanning*. The beam scans every point on the target, line by line, 30 times a second. Every second, 30 pictures are sent out of the camera tube.

As the beam of electrons moves across the target, each

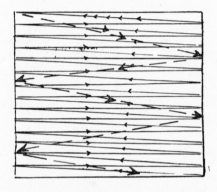

The beam scans the target something like this, but instead of just a few lines there are hundreds.

spot grabs back enough electrons to replace the ones it lost. When the stream bounces back from the target it varies exactly the way the waves of light that make up the picture varied when they came into the tube. When this varying beam of electrons returns to the plate, it is called the *signal*. It is a picture in electricity of the light picture that came into the tube.

The signal plate sends each electric signal out of the tube in order, and all the time the electron gun keeps scanning the target, picking up new pictures. The signals flow out of the orthicon to the grid of an amplifier, where they are magnified and sent on to the transmitter.

131

Here they are broadcast just as ordinary radio waves are, except that they are sent at higher frequencies. The electrical picture signal is called the *video* signal, and the sound that goes along with it is called the *audio* signal. Because television frequencies are so high, and the waves are so short, there is a great problem in television broadcasting. It is difficult to broadcast signals very far. Instead of being reflected from the ionized gas layer as ordinary radio waves are, television waves go right on through the layer and out into space. They do not bounce back to earth again. They travel only in straight lines, like light waves.

Television waves are very short. They will not bend around the earth, and they go right through the gas layers instead of bouncing off.

When the high-frequency waves that carry the television signals are picked up by the aerial of your receiving set, they are carried into the receiver and there they are rectified into a fluctuating direct current.

132

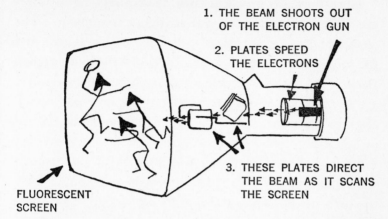

1. THE BEAM SHOOTS OUT
OF THE ELECTRON GUN

2. PLATES SPEED
THE ELECTRONS

3. THESE PLATES DIRECT
THE BEAM AS IT SCANS
THE SCREEN

FLUORESCENT
SCREEN

The most important part of the receiver is the cathode-ray tube, with an electron gun in its neck. The big end of the tube is a fluorescent screen.

The fluctuating beam of electrons shoots out of the gun and scans the fluorescent screen exactly as the beam in the orthicon does. Since this beam is made of little charges of electricity exactly like the ones that flowed out of the signal plate, it makes a picture on the screen that is built of thousands of little dots of light.

You see all these separate dots as a picture, and the thirty separate still pictures a second make one continuous moving picture, because your eyes can't work fast enough to see the spaces between the dots of light or the pictures. You are still seeing the light waves from one picture when the next one flashes along, and so you miss the space in between. If you don't see how a picture can be made this way, from dots of light, just look closely at any of the photographs in your morning newspaper. You will see that the whole picture is built of tiny dots.

Electronics Entertains You—Television

For years, many people have experimented with different methods for broadcasting in color, and so far the most practical method works like this.

In the color camera are three separate image orthicon tubes, and the camera lens focuses the picture onto them through a series of lenses and mirrors. The light rays go through colored filters so that the red parts of the picture are picked up by one tube, the blue by another, and the green by the last. Each tube converts the light rays it receives into electrical impulses which are amplified and transmitted just the way they are in black-and-white television. As a matter of fact, you can receive color as a black-and-white picture on your ordinary receiver.

The color tube in the receiver, which is called a *tricolor tube,* contains three electron guns instead of one. Each gun is worked by the electrical impulses from one of the camera tubes.

Each gun shoots its electron stream toward a plate at the flat end of the tube. This plate has been coated with thousands of groups of phosphor dots arranged in triangles of one red, one blue, and one green dot.

Between the electron guns and the phosphor plate is another plate, called the *aperture* or *shadow plate.* This plate has thousands of tiny holes, one for each group of colored dots on the phosphor plate.

The streams from the electron guns are focused so that they cross going through each hole in the aperture plate, on their way to the phosphor plate.

The stream from each gun hits its own color dot, making it glow, but is shadowed away from the other

134

Electronics Entertains You—Television

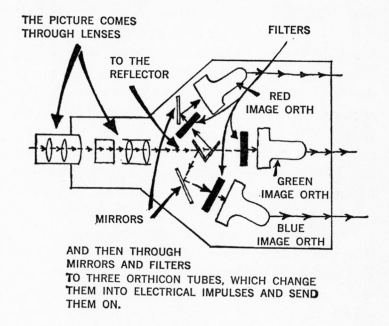

THE PICTURE COMES
THROUGH LENSES

FILTERS

TO THE
REFLECTOR

RED
IMAGE ORTH

GREEN
IMAGE ORTH

MIRRORS

BLUE
IMAGE ORTH

AND THEN THROUGH
MIRRORS AND FILTERS
TO THREE ORTHICON TUBES, WHICH CHANGE
THEM INTO ELECTRICAL IMPULSES AND SEND
THEM ON.

color dots in that group. The stronger the stream, the more brightly its dot glows. If the red dot were bright, the blue just glowing, and the green not even activated, that group would look purple.

The three guns scan the phosphor plate through every hole, just as the electron gun scans the fluorescent plate in a black-and-white tube. But now the picture is made of thousands of glowing colored dots, which you see as a color picture. If you wonder how all those dots can make a clear color picture, take a close and careful look at the color pictures in your favorite magazine.

135

THE TRICOLOR TUBE WORKS LIKE THIS

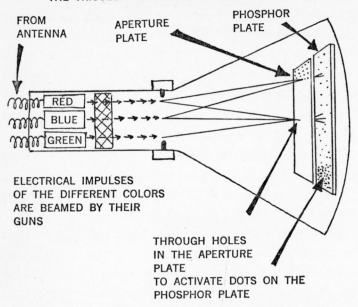

FROM ANTENNA

APERTURE PLATE

PHOSPHOR PLATE

RED
BLUE
GREEN

ELECTRICAL IMPULSES OF THE DIFFERENT COLORS ARE BEAMED BY THEIR GUNS

THROUGH HOLES IN THE APERTURE PLATE TO ACTIVATE DOTS ON THE PHOSPHOR PLATE

This color is transmitted on the ultra high-frequency wave lengths. There are several advantages in transmitting television over these ultra high-frequency bands.

Television transmission requires a very broad band of wave lengths to carry its full range of impulses. This limits the number of stations that can operate in any location without interfering with one another or with other broadcasting.

In the very high frequencies wave lengths are so much shorter that there is more room. Because of this, each television station can use more space and broadcast more elements to make a better picture, just as a magazine picture, which is made up of hundreds of thousands of dots, is clearer than a comic book picture which is made up of much fewer.

You can usually tell the difference between a "live" television picture, which is one that is being taken on the spot by a television camera, and a film. But many television programs are recorded on video tape, and you can't tell the difference between a video-tape recording and a live program.

Video-tape recording is a way of instantly transferring the picture that is being taken by a television camera onto magnetic tape. It does not have to be developed or processed in any way.

Video tape starts as a clear plastic tape, a lot like the kind you use around the house. It is then coated with iron oxide, which is magnetic and reacts to electrical impulses. The electrical signals from the television camera and the microphone form a magnetic pattern on the tape which can be played back instantly into a picture and sound.

A video tape recorder can record signals directly from a nearby television camera, or from a camera on location, or from signals from a studio thousands of miles away, as long as it is connected to that studio by cable. The tape retains the picture indefinitely, so it can be stored and used at any time. If the recording is no longer needed, the tape can be erased by magnetism and used over and over again.

A black-and-white recorder consists of a desklike *console* which holds the reels of tape, the recording devices and the controls. Two racks of electron tubes supply

A video tape recorder looks like this

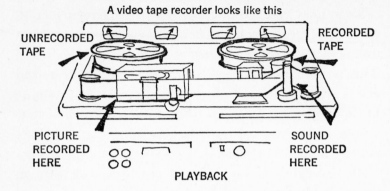

UNRECORDED TAPE

RECORDED TAPE

PICTURE RECORDED HERE

SOUND RECORDED HERE

PLAYBACK

the power for the different operations. The same equipment with additional racks of tubes can be used to record color television.

Because television waves travel in straight lines, only as far as the earth's curve, transmitters are usually located on top of very high buildings.

A relay system is often used for broadcasting over longer distances. A network of microwave relay stations placed on hills and mountains scoop the signals out of the air, strengthen them and send them on to the next station. These stations work automatically. Nobody has to be around to handle the equipment.

If television signals are being sent directly over very long distances they travel through a specially built cable called a *coaxial,* which also carries long-distance telephone calls. Coaxial cables are wires, suspended by insulators inside copper tubes which keep the signals from leaking away. Coaxial cables under the seas will connect the whole world by television, just as they do now by telephone.

Electronics Entertains You—Television

Sometimes you see on your television screen motion pictures of news events that have been sent over great distances by a process called *motion picture facsimile*. This is similar to the facsimile broadcasting we talked about in an earlier chapter. Motion picture facsimile broadcasting is a first step toward intercontinental television. It lets you see quickly something that just happened thousands of miles away on another continent.

The pictures on the film are not broadcast through the air, but are changed into electric signals and slowed down enough to travel through the telephone cable that runs under the sea.

Motion picture facsimile films look a little jumpy because the recorder only scans every other picture on the film. The signal to be transmitted is added to the carrier wave and transmitted at the rate of one picture every eight seconds. At the receiving end of the cable the picture signal comes into a cathode-ray tube which changes it back to light. Then the picture on the tube is re-recorded on film and played at the usual speed of 24 pictures a second.

Television receivers used to be big and bulky. The large number of tubes and the complicated wiring took up a lot of room. The sets had to be connected to antennas and to electrical outlets for power. Now there are television receivers that you can pick up with one hand and take wherever you want—even to the beach or into the woods.

The power comes from batteries. Transistors have replaced many of the tubes. The bulky, complicated wiring has been replaced by printed circuits. (Transistors and printed circuits are used in tiny radios too.)

Printed circuits have not only made small television and radio receivers possible, but have been a big step toward automation in the manufacture of these things. Ordinary wiring has to be done by hand. Now there is a way to actually print an electrical circuit. If you have a new radio or television set it might have one of these printed circuits. You can see it when the back is opened.

The base of the circuit is usually plastic board. One side is coated with a thin film of copper that will finally be the circuit. Over the copper is a coat of photographic emulsion, like that on a roll of film.

The diagram of the wiring circuit is printed onto the emulsion in a special, acid-resistant ink; then the whole board is dipped in an acid bath. The acid rinses away everything but the coated picture of the wiring. Then the ink is rinsed off too, leaving just the copper-wiring circuit printed on the board, ready to conduct electrons to their work.

Television has many other uses besides entertainment. You can read about its military uses in Chapter 16.

Television cameras in waterproof steel cases are exploring the seas. The cameras can be steered by remote

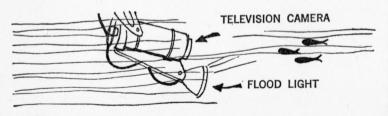

TELEVISION CAMERA

FLOOD LIGHT

control from a monitor ship. The cameras have motors for moving them through the water and for tilting them to any angle. These television cameras are used by oceanographers for studying the life and topography of the seas. They are also used for salvage operations. At depths where the sea begins to darken, brilliant floodlights are used.

Television cameras in rockets and satellites are exploring space and transmitting what they see back to observer stations on earth.

Sometime, maybe soon, television relay stations will be located on platforms in the sky, receiving their signals and even the power to operate from broadcasting stations on earth.

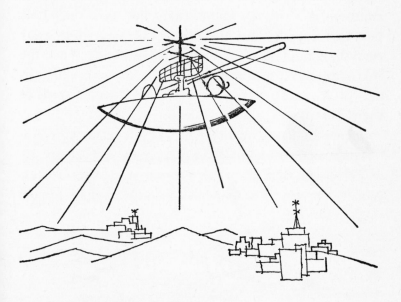

Chapter Sixteen
ELECTRONS FOR DEFENSE AND PEACE

WAR or a threat to a country's security hurry the development of many inventions that might otherwise take years to perfect. In an emergency a country's resources of brains and money seem unlimited. Many of the greatest strides we have made in electronics and atomic energy have been made under these conditions.

The most important uses of electronics in defense are communication, the gathering and passing on of information and control. All of these have an important place in our everyday lives too.

Electrons for Defense and Peace

Communication is very important. Command posts must keep in touch with all units under their control. Men in different parts of a plane or ship must be able to talk to one another. Orders must be given and received. Information must be relayed.

Communication means hundreds of thousands of radio transmitters and receivers at work. The "walkie-talkie" or two-way portable radio was a wartime development. It had to be light enough for a man to carry for hours and miles, yet powerful enough to be a complete broadcasting and receiving station wherever it was located.

There are many peacetime uses for these two-way radios. All police cars have them. Now they are in many private automobiles too. They connect those cars with telephones anywhere. A taxi company can phone its cabs. An emergency service can contact its repair trucks. The lady down the block can call her husband on his way home from the office and ask him to stop for a loaf of bread.

Ship-to-shore telephones are really radios too. Most of these two-way radio calls are not made direct, but through a special operator. They operate on a radio-frequency band of their own.

Railroad trains use two-way radios too. The men in the caboose can talk to the men in the engine without having to stop the train or walk the tops of forty or fifty freight cars that separate them.

When you think of all the amplifier and oscillator tubes in an ordinary broadcasting station, and the care that is taken to locate the high transmitting towers in exactly the right place, you can see that the tubes in a two-way radio really have their work cut out for them.

Another "radio soldier" is the navigational device that brings planes safely home on a radio beam. Pilots can follow the beam hundreds of miles to their home fields, through night and fog, even if their other navigation instruments are not working. The beam guides airplanes into unfamiliar airports too. The radio man only has to keep tuned to the frequency on which the beam is being broadcast.

Sometimes the beam is a sound tone the pilot hears through his earphones. If the tone wavers or stops, he knows he is "off the beam."

Another kind of radio-beam device is a dial which the pilot watches. It shows him when he is flying on course and when he goes off. A similar dial helps him to land even if he can't see the runway.

ON COURSE   OFF COURSE   CORRECT

LANDING
APPROACH

Radar was first developed for military use. Its job was to supply information. Radar is an intelligence expert. Bunches of very short, high-frequency waves, generated by a magnetron, are broadcast by the antenna. The interesting thing about radar is that the sending and receiving equipment are in the same place, so the waves go out, then come back and report.

The waves are sent out in intense little bunches, and after each bunch there is a pause. During the pause the receiver waits to hear the echo of the bunch that was just sent out. The echo that comes back is the reflection of the radar waves from any object they hit. There really isn't much waiting between bunches of waves. Since they travel 186,000 miles a second, if there is anything to reflect the wave the echo comes back in a fraction—perhaps just a few millionths—of a second. Since the senders know how fast the wave is traveling, they can tell from the time it takes the echo to get back exactly how far away the object is that reflected the waves.

Radar is sent out in every direction in a huge radio net that covers the air for miles around. The instant a plane (or even a piece of tinfoil) comes into the area that is protected by this net of waves, it reflects them back to the receiver.

Electrons for Defense and Peace

Radar impulses from airports or aircraft bases or ships are sent out in beams that scan the skies or waters just as a watchman would play a flashlight beam across a dark room where a burglar might be working. The whole antenna turns as it directs the beam, and then, if an echo comes back, the radar crew knows the exact location from which the "tracked" plane is coming.

An important part of radar is the indicator screen where the operator can see the beam. It usually looks like a single straight line, but as soon as it hits something and is reflected, the line develops jiggles. Those jiggles are the objects that are reflecting the beam. The operator can tell from their position on the line just where the target is.

Some kinds of radar screens show a different kind of picture. The beam looks almost like a windshield wiper, wiping across the screen. Only it wipes the picture on. Everything the beam touches reflects the fast-moving beam which scans it, and almost draws a map on the screen. Ships can see shorelines or other ships, and planes can see the ground over which they fly.

Although it was developed in war, radar has a great number of peacetime uses. All large ships and many small craft use it to guide them safely through narrow or unfamiliar channels and through fog. Radar tells them how close they are to other ships and to the shores and islands on either side.

Modern airports depend heavily on radar. It lets them see the minute-to-minute position of every plane approaching the airport, even when visibility is zero.

146

Electrons for Defense and Peace

The weather bureau uses radar to detect approaching storms and to tell just how far away they are. Radar helps airliners to avoid stormy spots too.

Radar does not locate submarines for radio waves cannot travel through water. Ships have special devices for locating submarines. These devices send out supersonic or ultrasonic waves; sound waves that are too short to be heard. The human ear can hear vibrations of from 16 to 16,000 times a second. Anything faster is ultrasonic and cannot be heard by man. Ultrasonic waves are easy to generate and easy to focus into a beam. They are made electrically and can be directed through the water under the ship.

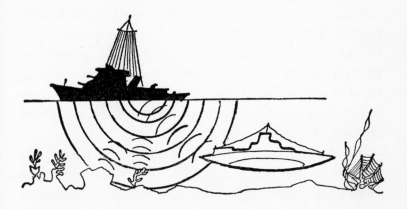

The waves are sent through the water in very short bunches. When they hit something they echo back to the ship. Since supersonic waves travel at the speed of ordinary sound waves, about 4,000 feet a second in water, the location of the object can be figured at once.

From this principle an electronic echo-sounding instrument has been developed that is so sensitive that it not only finds large or small submerged objects but can even locate fish.

These instruments are very helpful in making accurate maps of the ocean bottom which, in some places, is still only roughly charted.

Infra-red, too, plays an important part in the job of intelligence. Most objects reflect infra-red as well as wave lengths of visible light, and these infra-red wave lengths are much more penetrating. If the door to a furnace were closed you could not see the light of the fire inside because the wave lengths of light from the fire could not penetrate the iron furnace. But you could feel the heat of the infra-red waves coming right through the furnace walls. In the same way infra-red can penetrate fog, clouds and night.

Special films are sensitive to wave lengths of infra-red. Since everything has some heat in it, everything is always giving off infra-red rays. Film that is sensitive to infra-red will react to these rays just as ordinary film reacts to light, so pictures can be taken on this film from an airplane that is miles up in the air, through clouds or fog or darkness.

An airplane carrying special television broadcasting equipment combined with infra-red can broadcast directly to a ground receiver exactly what is happening on the ground below it. It can broadcast the progress of maneuvers or of a battle. It can broadcast the progress of a traffic jam, a forest fire or a flood.

148

Electrons for Defense and Peace

The job of gathering information works hand in hand with the job of communicating it. The information itself is of no use unless someone knows about it and can use it.

The science of *telemetering* is a wedding of both these jobs. Telemetering was developed along with rockets, when we needed eyes and ears and brains in space. Electronic devices measure radiations and temperature, a rocket's speed and heat and the air pressure around it. They observe the performance of instruments and radio all this information back to waiting ground observers.

Electrons for Defense and Peace

Control devices, too, work with instruments that gather and communicate information. Once all these jobs were done by human beings. Scouts gathered information. Messengers took it back to headquarters. The officer in charge considered the information, decided on his strategy and led his forces into action. Let's see how these jobs are done now by our air defense system, SAGE, which stands for Semi-Automatic Ground Environment.

At a SAGE command post, computers, many radios and radar devices are in constant operation. Information pours in steadily from manned and unmanned radar stations, from observers and ships and planes. The information is fed into computers where it is sorted and memorized and analyzed. If action is needed the computer decides which of many air bases is in the best position to defend or counterattack. It decides whether planes or missiles should be used.

If planes are sent, they are guided automatically to the target and then the pilots take over. But the computer is still at work keeping track of fuel supplies and alerting new units to action.

If the computer decides to use missiles, automation takes over there too. As information comes into the control room of the missile base, computers figure out the number of attackers, their present location, their course, speed and the best position to intercept them. Other computers decide which missiles to use, get them into position, fire and launch them at the exact spot decided upon. First, though, the computers check themselves to be sure that all their own parts have operated properly and haven't made any errors.

The computers themselves do *not* decide whether to defend or attack. This decision is made by human brains at a central command post where the reports from all the SAGE command posts funnel in.

SAGE sounds like a purely military operation, but it could be used to control commercial air traffic too.

All of the work we do with rockets and earth satellites is completely dependent on electronics. A satellite itself, at the present time, is simply a case full of tubes, wires and transistors. It has devices for measuring heat, speed and cosmic rays. It has guidance controls and generators for changing solar energy into electrical energy to run the radio equipment that telemeters information back to earth.

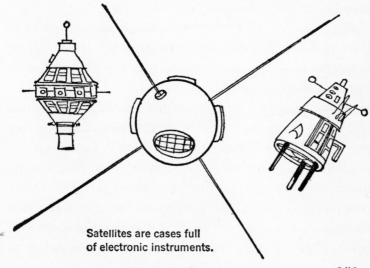

Satellites are cases full
of electronic instruments.

Electrons for Defense and Peace

Rockets are not quite so compact. They have tanks for fuel, engines for using it and room for the "payload" which is the reason for sending up the rocket. The payload may be a satellite or a nose cone carrying animals and equipment. In time of war it could be an atomic warhead. Soon it will be men, traveling in space.

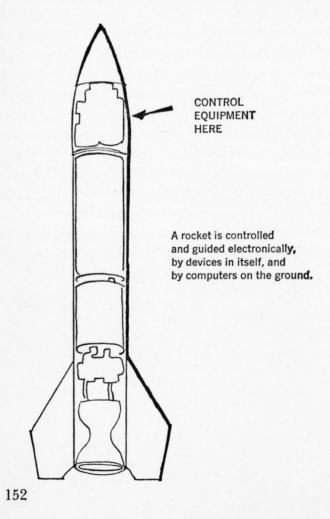

CONTROL
EQUIPMENT
HERE

A rocket is controlled
and guided electronically,
by devices in itself, and
by computers on the ground.

Electrons for Defense and Peace

Building and then launching a rocket is a complicated electronic job. It is guided every step of the way by computers which figure speeds, trajectories, stresses and strains, orbits and split seconds of firing. The computer tells if any of the millions of parts is not working right. Then the safety officer decides whether or not to destroy the rocket.

Every day thousands of scientists and engineers are at work perfecting and improving these controls. When the first travelers start into space they will actually be safer than Charles Lindbergh was on that first airplane flight across the Atlantic Ocean.

While it seems a shame that so many great inventions were originally developed for military use, it's a good thing for mankind that most of them can be adapted to make great strides for us in a world at peace. Robot bombs started us on the path of our exploration of space. The atomic bomb opened a whole new age in the world's history. It brought us into the era of atomic energy.

Chapter Seventeen
ATOMIC ENERGY

WHEN WE TALK about the power of atomic energy, we mean something different from the energy of electrons at work. Atomic energy is really nuclear energy. It is power released from the nucleus itself.

If scientists had not first found out about electrons and their nuclei, about how atoms are made, they could never have released atomic energy. If we did not have electronic equipment we could not work with atomic energy. Electronics, working in the field of atomic energy, does all its usual jobs: it figures and computes, it generates and converts, it controls, monitors, and signals.

The research that led to the secret of releasing nuclear energy moved along a somewhat different path than that which led us, earlier, into the field of electronics. It started with the discovery of X-rays by Professor Wilhelm Konrad Roentgen, in 1895. The scientific world was agog. What were these mysterious rays? Where did they come from and how were they created? Scientists everywhere took up the challenge and began experimenting with X-rays and ways to produce them.

Atomic Energy

At about the same time Professor Antoine Becquerel made the accidental discovery that the element uranium continually gave off rays of its own which behaved like X-rays.

Marie and Pierre Curie, a young couple who had been doing research in Professor Becquerel's laboratory, continued the experiments and made another astonishing discovery. Pitchblende, the ore from which the uranium was obtained, gave off rays that were much stronger than those of the pure uranium. After much patient work with the pitchblende, the Curies discovered a new element, two and a half million times stronger in these mysterious Becquerel rays than uranium. Radium was giving off these rays all the time—and nothing could stop it—rays that made the air around them electric, that created heat, that killed bacteria and other organisms, and that made things phosphorescent.

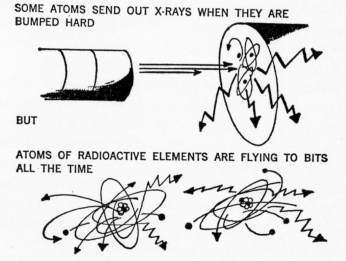

SOME ATOMS SEND OUT X-RAYS WHEN THEY ARE BUMPED HARD

BUT

ATOMS OF RADIOACTIVE ELEMENTS ARE FLYING TO BITS ALL THE TIME

Atomic Energy

We said in an early chapter that X-rays were created when the electrons in the target were hit so hard that they were shaken out of place. In their struggle to regain their positions, they sent off these powerful rays.

Atoms of uranium, radium, and the other elements that we call "radioactive" give off rays for a similar reason. They haven't been bumped, but they are naturally unstable, and are breaking down, bit by bit, all the time. In any bit of radium, for instance, some atoms are flying to pieces every second and shooting off waves of energy as they do.

J. J. Thomson and Lorentz came along with their electron theories even before radioactivity was discovered. They said from the beginning that these waves must be caused by some activity inside the atom itself—the atom they could no longer believe to be the smallest particle of matter.

In 1900, a German physics professor named Max Planck worked out a theory that an atom gives off energy not in a steady stream, but in short bursts that cannot be divided. He called these bursts or jerks of energy "quanta." Since Planck's idea has been proved, a wholly new kind of mathematical thinking, called the quantum theory, has been built on this discovery.

In 1900, Ernest Rutherford, who studied under Thomson, made another important discovery. He analyzed the rays that were given off by radium and found that there were really three different kinds. He called them *alpha*, *beta*, and *gamma* rays. They all come from the nucleus of the atom.

Atomic Energy

THE GAMMA RAYS ARE VERY SHORT X-RAYS

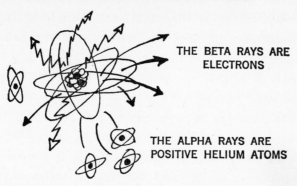

THE BETA RAYS ARE ELECTRONS

THE ALPHA RAYS ARE POSITIVE HELIUM ATOMS

The gamma rays were exactly like X-rays, but shorter in wave length. They are also *radiant energy*.

The beta rays were streams of electrons. And the alpha rays were streams of particles with a positive charge. But they were not just protons! They were whole helium atoms—two electrons, two protons, and two neutrons—the whole thing carrying a positive charge. These helium atoms are part of the nuclei of many elements.

We said before that an atom of one element is different from an atom of another only because of the difference in the number and arrangement of electrons around the nucleus of that atom, balancing the number of protons in the nucleus.

The number of electrons rotating around the nucleus of every atom determines the *atomic number* of the element. For instance, hydrogen has one electron, so it is number one, while uranium has ninety-two, so that is its number.

The protons and neutrons in the nucleus are what de-

157

termine the *atomic weight* of an element, which is something different from the atomic number, even though
these weights go up the scale in the same general order
that the atomic numbers do.

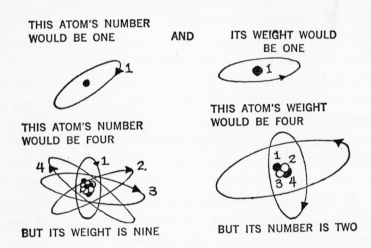

THIS ATOM'S NUMBER
WOULD BE ONE   AND   ITS WEIGHT WOULD
                                            BE ONE

THIS ATOM'S NUMBER
WOULD BE FOUR

THIS ATOM'S WEIGHT
WOULD BE FOUR

BUT ITS WEIGHT IS NINE   BUT ITS NUMBER IS TWO

Electrons weigh so little that they aren't even counted
in the atomic weight. So the weight of an atom is made
up of the protons and neutrons (which weigh about the
same) in its nucleus. Atoms with a lot of protons and
neutrons in their nuclei are very heavy (for atoms),
while atoms with just a few are very light.

Sometimes, for reasons we'll talk about later, it is important for scientists to know how many neutrons there
are in an atom, and they can find out with a little simple
arithmetic. Again let's take hydrogen, for example. Its
atomic number is one, so it has one electron circling the
nucleus, and of course, one proton to balance it in the
nucleus. But its atomic weight is just a fraction over one

unit, so there cannot be any neutrons in the nucleus. If there were even one, it would weigh at least two.

But uranium, with 92 electrons, weighs a little more than 238 units. Two hundred and thirty-eight minus the 92 protons in the nucleus leaves 146 neutrons.

Well, Rutherford discovered that when uranium atoms lost alpha particles, which were protons and neutrons, from their nuclei, and then lost the electrons that balanced them, they actually turned into elements of lower and lower atomic weight and number. Gradually, uranium would become radium, and radium would become lead. The elements themselves were changing, which was something that had always been thought impossible by all but the old alchemists, dreaming in their magic shops.

In 1919 Rutherford smashed the first atom, and discovered something else of tremendous importance. When he bombarded atoms of nitrogen with alpha particles given off by radium, the protons that shot out of the smashed atoms had greater energy than the alpha particles that released them. In other words, in smashing an atom, Rutherford was using a little energy to release a great deal more.

He was beginning to prove the theory that Professor Einstein had advanced fourteen years before, that matter and energy are the same thing in different costumes, and that one could be changed to the other. He said that when a body speeds up, it gets heavier. Some of its energy turns into matter. And a very small amount of matter can be changed into an enormous amount of energy. Einstein said that if you could release *all* the energy in any amount

of matter (we call it "mass") you would have an amount
of energy that equaled

> the mass
> multiplied by the speed of light (186,000 miles a
> second)
> multiplied again by 186,000.

So the amount of energy released would be staggering, if
the whole mass could be changed into energy. The first
atomic bomb, which was the greatest release of energy
the world had ever known, released the energy of only
one-tenth of one per cent of the matter used. The explosion of one uranium atom releases more than six billion
times the energy shot into it.

When Rutherford smashed his nitrogen atoms, he
didn't do it by aiming the alpha particles at them the
way you would shoot a gun at a tiger. He just put a bit of
radium salts, which were giving off alpha particles all the
time, into a tube with some nitrogen gas and hoped the
alpha particles would make accidental hits on the atoms

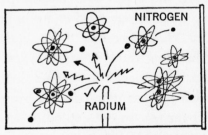

**RUTHERFORD'S ATOM-SMASHING
EXPERIMENT**

of nitrogen. It was like firing a gun into a pitch-black jungle, hoping some tigers would get in the way.

Now the job of the scientists was to build atom-smashers in which they could aim particles at the atoms, and smash them when they wanted to. This was easier to plan than to do. The atom-smashers were giant machines, and the energy it took to produce and fire the atom-smashing particles was far greater than the energy released from the direct hits, which were few and far between. A million particles had to be fired to get one direct hit on a nucleus. It was the same old job of shooting tigers in a dark jungle. They did discover, though, that they got far better results using neutrons, instead of alpha particles, for ammunition. That is because the neutrons are neutral and do not need as much energy to get by the electrons going around each atom. And when they slowed the neutrons down, better still.

The atom-smashing experiments proved that Einstein's theory was right. The energy released from each smashed atom was enormous. But since so few atoms were hit, what was needed was a way to make the particles from each exploding nucleus smash other atoms around them. This is called a "chain reaction."

In a way, the same thing happens when you hold a match to a piece of paper. You may set only one corner on fire, but each part, as it burns, sets fire to the paper around it. A chain reaction of exploding atoms does the same thing. The particles shooting out from the nucleus of each smashed atom smash other atoms around them.

Atomic Energy

THIS NEUTRON EXPLODES A NUCLEUS

AND THE FLYING NEUTRONS FROM THAT ATOM, AS IT EXPLODES, HIT OTHER NUCLEI AND EXPLODE THEM

And as the nucleus of an atom splits, energy is released. This is the tremendous mysterious energy we talked about in Chapter 1, the energy that has been binding all the protons and neutrons in the nucleus together all the time. The energy released in the breaking of a uranium atom is about five million times more than that released in one of the ways we use now—the burning of coal.

So one way of releasing nuclear power (which is what atomic power really is) is to split an atom of a heavy element apart into two lighter elements. This is called *fission*.

Another way would be to bind lighter elements together into a heavier one. Often the weight of a heavier nucleus is less than the weight of two lighter ones added together. This means that the extra mass is given off as energy when they combine. This process is called *fusion*.

162

Atomic Energy

The vast energy of the sun is created by fusion as hydrogen atoms are forced together under tremendous pressure to form helium atoms. This is also the way the H bomb (or hydrogen bomb) creates its energy.

FUSION WORKS LIKE THIS

LIGHTER ELEMENTS ARE FORCED TOGETHER UNDER IMMENSE PRESSURES TO FORM A HEAVIER ONE.

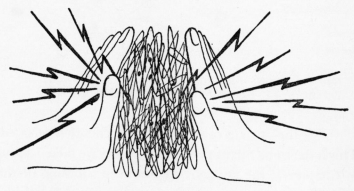

WHEN THE WEIGHT OF THE COMBINED NUCLEUS IS LESS THAN THAT OF THE TWO LIGHTER ONES TOGETHER, THE EXTRA MASS IS GIVEN OFF AS ENERGY.

But for a reason we'll discuss in a moment, most nuclear energy released by man's efforts is released through fission. A heavy atom is broken apart into two lighter ones.

This is done by shooting a neutron at the nucleus of the atom, but not so fast that it will whizz past or through the nucleus and continue on its way. The neutron must be going slowly enough for the nucleus to throw out a net and capture it.

Atomic Energy

FISSION WORKS LIKE THIS

A SLOW NEUTRON LANDS IN THE NUCLEUS

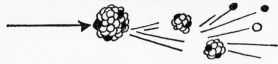

AND SPLITS IT INTO TWO MUCH LIGHTER NUCLEI
AND
THE LOST MASS IS TRANSFORMED INTO ENERGY

When an atom captures a neutron, one of two things happens. In most cases its atomic weight changes, even though it remains an atom of the same element, having the same number of electrons and protons in it. Now it is called an *isotope*. If it loses a neutron it is an isotope too. Almost every element has its isotopes—atoms that have the same atomic number as normal atoms but a different weight because there are more or less neutrons in their nuclei.

Some isotopes are unstable. They break down more easily than their brother atoms of normal weight. Scientists experimenting with the isotope of uranium that weighed 235 instead of the usual 238 discovered the second thing an atom can do when a neutron lands in its nucleus. It can split into two much lighter elements, releasing a tremendous amount of the energy that was needed to bind such a heavy nucleus together. And when it splits, the nucleus shoots out several neutrons that will split other atoms.

This is the important chain reaction that must happen to release any large amount of nuclear power.

164

Atomic Energy

But U235 is very difficult to make from ordinary uranium. Besides, 140 pounds of ordinary uranium contain only one pound of U235. Scientists decided to use these little amounts of U235 to produce greater amounts of another element that would serve as well.

When the neutrons released by the fission of U235 hit atoms of ordinary U238, those atoms, instead of splitting, each capture a neutron and become another isotope, U239. But U239 is unstable, and soon it shoots out an electron. When this happens, something odd occurs. A neutron changes into a proton. This makes many scientists believe that a neutron is really a proton and an electron fused together. Now a new element has been created with 93 protons.

This element isn't stable either, and it shoots out another beta particle, or electron. Another neutron changes into a proton, so that now there are 94. This new element, which is called plutonium, can be created in much greater amounts than U235, and a little U235 can be used to make a lot of plutonium. And a plutonium nucleus, when hit by a neutron, doesn't change into an isotope or another element. It breaks in two, just like a nucleus of U235.

In their study of the atom, scientists have many devices to help them.

They have atom smashers to break atoms apart so scientists can find out more about them.

They have cloud chambers where they can study the "tracks" of atomic particles to see how they behave.

165

Atomic Energy

They have spectrographs which weigh and sort atoms. They have atomic piles in which they can shoot neutrons at atoms until a chain reaction takes place. An atomic pile, or reactor, is built in such a way that a chain reaction can be controlled. By sliding carbon rods in and out the reaction can be started, slowed down or stopped.

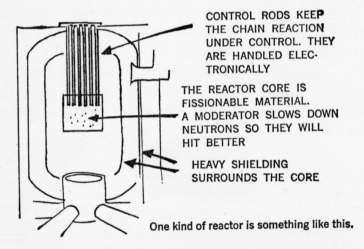

CONTROL RODS KEEP THE CHAIN REACTION UNDER CONTROL. THEY ARE HANDLED ELECTRONICALLY

THE REACTOR CORE IS FISSIONABLE MATERIAL. A MODERATOR SLOWS DOWN NEUTRONS SO THEY WILL HIT BETTER

HEAVY SHIELDING SURROUNDS THE CORE

One kind of reactor is something like this.

Actually a reactor is simpler than the simplest gasoline engine. Its only moving parts are the control rods. Pumps and valves work with it, but are not a part of the engine itself.

The radioactivity from a reactor is immense and very dangerous. It is the same kind of radioactivity created by the explosion of an atomic bomb. Weeks, months or even years later this radioactivity could kill anyone who had been exposed to it. Direct exposure would mean instant death.

The controls of a nuclear reactor must be handled

from a distance through thick shields, and many kinds of automation devices are used. Push button "hands" handle tools. Closed-circuit television watches every part of the operation. Radiation detectors inspect the workers to see if they have come in contact with even the slightest radiation. Different circuits inspect for different kinds of radiation.

Once the reactor is in operation, nothing inside can ever be touched again. If any repairs are necessary they must be made electronically, by remote control. Even the waste from a reactor is dangerous. It is encased in thick steel boxes which are then embedded in concrete blocks and dumped in the sea depths or buried far under the earth.

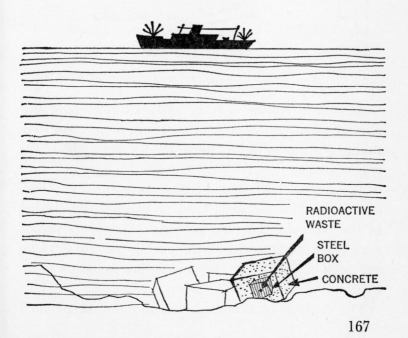

RADIOACTIVE WASTE

STEEL BOX

CONCRETE

Atomic Energy

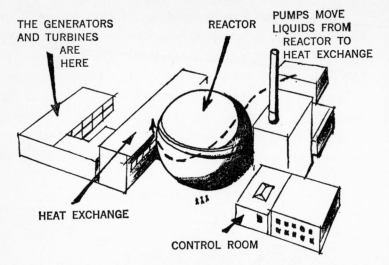

THE GENERATORS AND TURBINES ARE HERE

REACTOR

PUMPS MOVE LIQUIDS FROM REACTOR TO HEAT EXCHANGE

HEAT EXCHANGE

CONTROL ROOM

In a number of places reactors are used to generate the power that is used in homes and factories. But the power from a fission reactor cannot be used directly. Its energy appears as tremendous heat which makes steam to drive the turbines that generate electricity. This seems like a lot of trouble, but the amount of power released from a tiny bit of fissionable material is so great that reactors are worth the trouble and expense.

Some day we will have fusion reactors which will be more practical. Their fuel will be deuterium, an isotope of hydrogen which is plentiful in all the seas and waters of the world. The energy from fusion does not have to be converted. It acts just the way magnetism does in a generator, driving ions back and forth and causing electric current to flow in a coil around the reactor. Besides, fusion does not produce intense radioactivity as fission does.

Atomic Energy

The great problem in building a fusion reactor is in containing the tremendous heat needed to make fusion take place—as much as a hundred-million degrees. At this temperature any known material evaporates into gas.

Scientists think the answer will be a container of magnetism. They call it a "magnetic bottle." A strong magnetic field will ionize the atoms and hold them in place better than any kind of solid container could. And as

A "magnetic bottle" might work like this

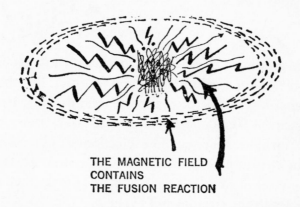

THE MAGNETIC FIELD
CONTAINS
THE FUSION REACTION

you remember, magnetism can be used to direct ions— it could even squeeze them together enough to heat them to the point of fusion.

Atomic power would make future wars very terrible, but it might also make them unnecessary. Many wars begin over the possession of a greater part of the raw materials of the world—the oil, coal or iron, the fertile soil, the waterways or the precious minerals. If, through atomic energy, unlimited amounts of power were avail-

169

able to all countries, nobody would have to fight over them. Enough power could be released from a cup of water to run an ocean liner. A snowball could supply the power for a great generator, an airplane could run on air.

There would be enough power to mine the precious metals out of the ocean, to fertilize and irrigate all the land in the world and to provide everything needed for good living, cheaply, for all the people in the world.

Not only is the power we generate in reactors important, but so are the radioactive isotopes which are a by-product of atomic energy. Another name for these is *tracers,* because with them we can trace the mysterious things that happen in plants or animals, in metals and chemicals, in our own bodies. This is because the isotopes can be tracked by a Geiger counter.

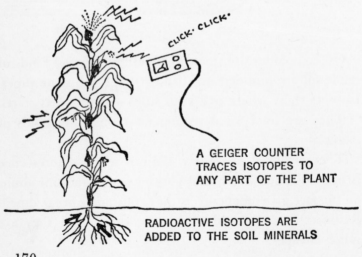

CLICK· CLICK·

A GEIGER COUNTER
TRACES ISOTOPES TO
ANY PART OF THE PLANT

RADIOACTIVE ISOTOPES ARE
ADDED TO THE SOIL MINERALS

Atomic Energy

If you eat radioactive salt, for example, the Geiger counter can trace that salt to any part of your body. Doctors can see exactly how your body uses different foods, vitamins, minerals or medicines.

Plant scientists can trace the use of soil minerals by plants.

Industry has many uses for radioactive isotopes. Steel manufacturers use them to measure the temperature of molten steel and detect flaws in castings.

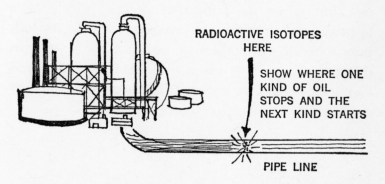

RADIOACTIVE ISOTOPES HERE

SHOW WHERE ONE KIND OF OIL STOPS AND THE NEXT KIND STARTS

PIPE LINE

Oil companies use them in pipelines. Several kinds of crude oil are pumped, in turn, through the same pipes. Isotopes show where one kind stops and the next starts.

They are used for detecting wear on many kinds of material.

They are used to replace radium where fluorescence is needed. Your watch dial glows because radium atoms on the face give off energy as they constantly break down. Radioactive isotopes do the same thing, and they are much cheaper.

Atomic Energy

Atomic power is beginning to do the things that oil, coal and water power have done until now. Big reactors supply everyday power. Small reactors run generators which supply electricity and heat to isolated outposts.

An atomic battery has been developed that could supply, without any outside connection, all the power needed in an ordinary household for many years. Some day a pebble of uranium or one of the new elements might be built into your car or airplane on the assembly line and you will never have to refuel.

Chapter Eighteen
SOMETHING NEW
EVERY MINUTE

During the time this book was being written, scientists were inventing new electronic devices, experimenting with new ways of using nuclear energy, proving or disproving new theories. While this book was being printed plans and experiments were announced that seemed like science fiction. After this book is printed there will be more. In electronics and atomics there is something new every minute.

There is an atomic clock which measures time even more accurately than the "old-fashioned" way. The atomic clock is accurate to within 3 seconds in a century. In working with atoms that travel at almost the speed of light, millionths of a second are very important.

A machine can reproduce electronically any tone or combination of tones that might be imagined by the human mind. A whole concert could be made up electronically without a single musical instrument, and recorded on a special roll of punched tape. You might even hear notes and chords that no instrument in the world is capable of playing.

Your house of the future will be an electronic miracle.

Something New Every Minute

Engineers have discovered that when current flows from one metal to another there are changes in temperature. Using this idea they have built air-conditioning panels thinner than walls that can heat or cool your house at the flick of a switch, depending on which side of the panel you have "on." Refrigerators use the same system.

Your house can be electronically dusted and cleaned and the air purified. Clothes, hung on their hangers in special closets, can be dry-cleaned or washed and dried right there. Stoves are operated from miles away, to cook dinners in minutes. Dishwashers have been built that wash, dry and put away the dishes. Ironers can also fold and stack the clothes.

Electronic supermarkets will make shopping a push-button job—unless, of course, you prefer to shop by television.

Automobiles on some highways will be electronically controlled by cables built beneath the road. Speed, passing and safety will be automatic. Special devices will warn of intersections and exits so you can change roads.

Some day air travel will be entirely controlled from the ground by computers, television observers, radar and automatic pilots.

Platforms stationed in the sky, perhaps six miles above the earth, would relay television and radio signals, make weather reports, keep track of shipping and even act as lighthouses marking cities around the world. They would be like fixed helicopters, getting the power to turn their rotors from batteries of amplitron tubes beamed at them from the ground.

174

Something New Every Minute

Because of our exploration of the atom we are on the threshold of new knowledge of ourselves and our world. We have unlimited sources of power. We have started into space. Every day our world becomes more exciting with new paths opening in many directions. We cannot see yet where they will lead, or who will be the explorers of the future. Perhaps you will be one.

ELECTRONIC TERMS
(and some atomic ones)

ALPHA PARTICLE. A positive particle released by the nucleus of an exploding atom. It is itself an atom of helium.

ALPHA RAY. A stream of alpha particles.

ALTERNATING CURRENT. Electric current that flows first one way and then the other in regular cycles.

AMPLIFY. To increase the strength of electric current without changing its pattern.

AMPLITRON. A tube for generating great amounts of microwave energy.

ANODE. The positive plate that pulls on the electrons in a vacuum tube.

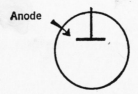

APERTURE PLATE. A plate punched with many holes for use in a tricolor television tube.

ATOM. The little universe that is made of electrons and their nucleus.

ATOM-SMASHER. A device for breaking atoms apart.

ATOMIC ENERGY. The total energy in an atom. Only a little is released by fission.

176

Electronic Terms (and some atomic ones)

ATOMIC NUMBER. The atomic number is equal to the number of electrons revolving around the nucleus of an atom. The atomic number determines the place of that atom in the scale of elements. Hydrogen with one electron is number one, uranium with 92 electrons is number 92.

ATOMIC PILE. A device for setting up a controlled chain reaction. (Also called a reactor.)

ATOMIC WEIGHT. The weight of an atom, expressed as the sum of the protons and neutrons in its nucleus.

AUDIO SIGNAL. Sound that has been changed into an electric impulse.

AUDIO-FREQUENCY WAVES. Radio waves that are as long as sound waves.

AUTOMATION. Electronic and mechanical control of a process.

BETA PARTICLES. Electrons released by a disintegrating atom.

BETA RAY. A stream of beta particles.

CARRIER WAVE. A radio wave that carries audio and video signals.

CATHODE. The part of an electron tube from which electrons are freed.

CATHODE-RAY TUBE. An electron tube in which the electrons flow in a ray or beam.

CHAIN REACTION. The breaking apart of other atoms by the particles released from the nucleus of an exploding atom during fission.

CIRCUIT. The complete path of an electric current.

Electronic Terms (and some atomic ones)

COLLECTOR. The part of a transistor which attracts electrons.

COMPUTER. An "electronic brain."

CONDENSER. A reservoir that stores charges of electricity.

CONDUCTOR. Anything through which electric current moves.

COSMIC RAYS. Particles of matter traveling through space at almost the speed of light, with immense energy and penetrating power.

CYCLE. One complete vibration of an electromagnetic wave.

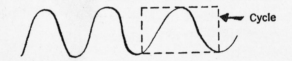

DIODE. An electron tube with just a cathode and an anode.

DIRECT CURRENT. Electric current that flows one way only.

EDISON EFFECT. The flow of electrons across a vacuum tube from the cathode to the anode.

ELECTRODES. The metal parts of a vacuum tube.

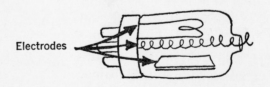

ELECTROMAGNETIC FORCE. A combination of electric and magnetic force.

ELECTRON. A minute particle of negative electricity.

ELECTRON GUN. An enclosed cathode out of which electrons are shot in a strong beam.

ELECTRON TUBE. The tube in which electrons are put to work.

ELECTRONICS. The science of putting the electron to work.

ELEMENTS. The simplest forms of matter, combinations of which form all other kinds of matter.

ENERGY. The ability to do work. *Kinetic* energy is that power while it is being used and *potential* energy is the power stored up and waiting.

ENVELOPE. The shell of an electron tube.

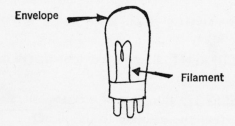

FILAMENT. A thin wire cathode that is heated directly or used to heat another cathode.

FILTER. A device for straining out all but a particular electromagnetic wave.

FISSION. The breaking in two of the nucleus of an atom, thus releasing energy.

Electronic Terms (and some atomic ones)

FLUCTUATE. To move like a wave, to vary and change.

FLUORESCENT. Able to give off radiations of its own while it is absorbing radiations from another source.

FREQUENCY. The number of cycles of electric current or electromagnetic waves in a second.

FRICTION. The rubbing of one thing against another.

FUSION. The combination of two lighter elements as they combine into a heavier one.

GAMMA RAYS. The most dangerous and penetrating radiations we know. Very high-voltage X-rays can be gamma rays, and the short rays that radium give off are gamma rays.

GEIGER COUNTER. A gas-filled tube and circuit which detects radioactivity.

GENERATOR. A machine that changes one kind of energy to another.

GRID. The part of an electron tube that controls the flow of electrons between the cathode and the anode.

GRID BIAS. The negative charge in the grid.

HIGH-VACUUM. Anything from which all possible air has been taken.

INFRA-RED. Electromagnetic radiations with wave lengths just longer than those of visible light.

INSULATOR. A very poor conductor of electric current.

ION. A gas atom that has had one or more of its electrons knocked out and is positive, or that has extra electrons and is negative.

IONIZE. To knock electrons out of gas atoms or add to them.

Electronic Terms (and some atomic ones)

IONOSPHERE. The layer of electrically charged gases that surrounds the earth at a height of 30 to 250 miles.

ISOTOPE. An atom of an element which has more or less neutrons in its nucleus than atoms of that element usually have, thus changing its atomic weight.

MAGNETIC FIELD. The magnetic area around a magnet or a conductor carrying electricity.

Magnetic field

MAGNETRON. A tube which uses magnetism to control the flow of electrons.

MATTER. The stuff of which everything in the world is made.

MEDIUM. Any substance through which a wave travels to get somewhere else.

MINIATURIZATION. The science of building always-smaller, practical electronic devices.

MODULATE. To mix the fluctuating signal that was made in the microphone with the wave that is going to carry it.

MOLECULE. The smallest amount of any kind of matter that can be recognized as that particular kind of matter.

NEUTRON. Part of the nucleus that is neither positive nor negative.

NUCLEAR ENERGY. Energy released from the nucleus of an atom.

NUCLEUS. The positive center of an atom, around which the electrons move.

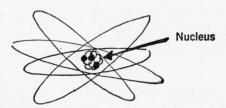

Nucleus

OSCILLATION. A complete vibration of a wave.

OSCILLATOR TUBE. An electron tube that makes alternating current.

PENTODE. An electron tube with five electrodes.

PHOSPHOR PLATE. A plate covered with dots of colored phosphors, used in a tricolor television tube.

PHOSPHORS. Powders that are fluorescent.

PHOTOSENSITIVE. Affected by light.

PHOTOTUBE. An electron tube in which light is changed into electricity.

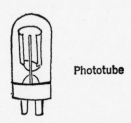

Phototube

PLATE. The positively charged anode in an electron tube to which electrons are drawn.

PLATE CURRENT. The flow of electrons from the circuit to the plate, or anode.

Electronic Terms (and some atomic ones)

POSITRON. An electron-like particle with a positive charge.

POTENTIAL. The difference between two charges of electricity which makes one flow to the other.

PROTON. A positively charged particle in the nucleus of an atom.

QUANTA. Indivisible bursts of energy given off by an atom.

RADIANT ENERGY. Waves or rays of energy.

RADIATION. Energy, transmitted as waves.

RADIOACTIVE ISOTOPE. An unstable isotope which emits radiations as it breaks down.

REACTOR. A device for the controlled changing of nuclear energy into a more useful form of energy.

RECTIFY. To change alternating current into direct current.

RESISTANCE. The struggle by atoms in a conductor to keep free electrons from flowing past them through the conductor.

SCAN. To cover a sensitive surface point by point and in order, with light or electrons.

SHADOW PLATE. See Aperture Plate.

SIGNAL PLATE. The plate behind the mosaic in a television camera tube, out of which the signals flow in order.

SIGNAL VOLTAGE. The voltage coming into the grid of an electron tube that controls the electrons flowing across the tube.

SOURCE. The place in the electron tube from which the electrons come.

SPACE CHARGE. The space around the cathode that is filled with a cloud of electrons in a vacuum tube, or with positive ions in a gas-filled tube.

SPECTROGRAPH. A device for weighing and sorting atoms.

STATIC ELECTRICITY. Electricity that is not moving in a current or that is made by rubbing two unlike things together.

SUPERSONIC WAVES. Sound waves that are too short to be heard by the human ear.

TARGET. A special place on an anode where an electron beam is supposed to hit.

TELEMETERING. An electronic system of sending messages from a rocket or other unmanned aircraft to a special receiving station.

TERMINALS. The prongs on an electron tube that connect the parts of the tube with their circuits.

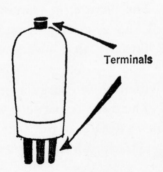

Terminals

TETRODE. An electron tube with four electrodes.

TRACER. A radioactive isotope. (Also called *trace element.*)

Electronic Terms (and some atomic ones)

TRANSISTOR. A small metal device which performs the function of an electron tube.

TRICOLOR TUBE. The receiving tube in a color television set.

TRIODE. An electron tube with a cathode, an anode, and a grid.

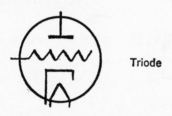

Triode

ULTRAVIOLET. Radiations with wave lengths just shorter than visible light.

VACUUM. Any space from which most of the air has been removed.

VIBRATION. The motion of a wave.

VIDEO SIGNAL. The picture, in television, after it has been changed into an electrical impulse.

VOLTAGE. The pressure that makes electric current flow.

WAVE. A single vibration of energy in motion.

WAVE LENGTH. The distance between two waves, from the top of one to the top of the next.

X-RAY. A very penetrating electromagnetic ray.

INDEX

Index

Index

Index

Index

ABOUT THE AUTHOR-ARTIST

Jeanne Bendick has written and illustrated a great number of books, including many leading science books. She is known everywhere in the children's book field for her ability to explain and illustrate difficult concepts and machines in a simple, graphic way. Her own books include ALL AROUND YOU, WHAT COULD YOU SEE? and HAVE A HAPPY MEASLE (with Candy and Rob Bendick, Jr.) for young readers; and for teenage readers—HOW MUCH AND HOW MANY, TELEVISION WORKS LIKE THIS (written with her husband, Robert Bendick), and ELECTRONICS FOR YOUNG PEOPLE.

In addition, she has illustrated such well-known books as Dorothy Canfield Fisher's A FAIR WORLD FOR ALL; Lynn Poole's TODAY'S SCIENCE AND YOU; Glenn Blough's THE TREE ON THE ROAD TO TURNTOWN, NOT ONLY FOR DUCKS, WAIT FOR THE SUNSHINE, LOOKOUT FOR THE FOREST, AFTER THE SUN GOES DOWN, WHO LIVES IN THIS HOUSE? and SOON AFTER SEPTEMBER; Herman Schneider's EVERYDAY MACHINES AND HOW THEY WORK, EVERYDAY WEATHER AND HOW IT WORKS, SCIENCE FUN WITH MILK CARTONS, and YOUR TELEPHONE AND HOW IT WORKS; Julius Schwartz's THROUGH THE MAGNIFYING GLASS; George Barr's YOUNG SCIENTIST TAKES A WALK, and many, many more.

A native New Yorker, she now lives with her husband and their two children in Rye, New York.

DATE DUE			
4-9-63	1-2-64	2/25/65	1-16-67
5-2-63	2-10-64	3/8/66	2-21-67
5-29-63	2-17-64	3-15-65	3-28-67
10-2-63	2-27-64	3-18-65	11-27-67
10-16-63	3-2-64	3-25-65	2-13-68
11-14-63	3-5-64	11-2-65	3-26-68
11-21-64	4-9-64	11-77-65	5-5-69
12-9-63	4-13-64	2-9-65	5-13-70
12/12/63	4-22-64	3-16-65	4-26-71
1-13-64	1-18-65	1/31/66	5-7-71
1-23-64	2/15/65	2-21/66	MAR 7 1972
		3-31-66	APR 10 1976